REMOVE BEFORE FLIGHT

By Captain Laura Einsetler

Dear Genie,
I hope you enjoy this book and may you always have smooth rides! So happy we can be friends through your man!
Love, ☺
Laura

Copyright

Copyright © 2012 by Laura Krista Einsetler

All rights reserved. This book or any portion thereof may not be reproduced or used in any manner whatsoever without the express written permission of the author except for the use of brief quotations in a book review.

First Publishing, 2017

ISBN 978-1-365-69433-2

Table of Contents

Copyright 2

Preface 4

Acknowledgement 6

Introduction 7

History 18

The Jets 25

Pilots 46

Planning to Fly 66

What the Flight Attendants Tell You and Why 76

Airline Operations 86

Safety and Security 101

The Weather 114

Travel Health 129

Preface

This book is dedicated to you, the aviation passenger. For all of the friendly smiles, looks of respect, thoughtfully asked questions, and interesting conversations that I have experienced, this is my gift back to you!

The very idea of this work came from a touching and engaging conversation I had with a passenger not too long ago. We discussed our lovely children, aspects of health, and specifics of flight. After I mentioned that I was working on a book primarily about my son called *Lost and Found*, detailing my struggles and experiences, he offered the idea of possibly writing another book for people like himself. He went on to explain that he travels often, mostly for business, but never quite feels comfortable with flying. I was thrilled at the prospect of helping so many people by sharing information and experience that I have built throughout the years as a pilot, a woman, a mother, and a friend.

The subject material that you will read comes from a compilation of questions, inquiries, and concerns expressed by many air travelers. My goal has been to address each item, dissect it, and explain it so that some of the mysteries of air travel may become clearer for you. This will help in your understanding of the environment in which you are traveling. It will make you feel empowered and confident as you take to the skies. Sit back, relax, and enjoy the ride!

Acknowledgement

To all of the mentors, instructors, pilots, friends, and family who believed in me, you gave me the strength and courage to push through and persevere during the challenges and difficult times in my life. I thank you with all that I am for all that you have given me. I cherish every moment, every memory, and every experience. To my most precious blessings Erik, Krista, and Frank, I love you bigger than the whole wide universe, and you are my meaning in this life. And to God, I give you my deepest gratitude for helping me always keep the blue side up!

"There is only one happiness in life, to love and to be loved." - George Sand

Introduction

So often we get to sit back, relax, and just enjoy the privilege of flying on a commercial airliner. We sip our drinks, tap away on a tablet computer, slide on the headphones, and maybe even drift off to sleep while we sail across the skies. This is the way to travel.

It becomes so routine, even for the most occasional traveler, that we have almost come to expect things to be always smooth and pleasant. But sometimes that dreamy experience is interrupted, even shattered. Maybe it's a roll through some moderate turbulence, maybe it's that ferocious lightning storm in central Texas, or another blizzard in Chicago. Or perhaps it's the captain coming over the intercom, saying "there is a problem with the airplane, so your flight is going to return to the airport."

Even those sounds that the airplane makes: whirrs, clunks, and Morse code bing-bongs that the flight crew send back and forth to each other. What's happening? So many little things can break a person's confidence, give just a second of fear, or make you doubt, despite all your good experiences and the favorable statistics, that everything will be fine.

My intention for creating this book is to help remove those fleeting moments of concern and unease. If I can answer some of these deep-seated questions in the back of your mind, perhaps you will feel more empowered and relaxed when you take to the skies. In fact, my goal is for you to have the most enjoyable and pleasurable flying experience possible.

From Me to You

Who am I to tell you these things? My name is Laura Einsetler, and I'm a commercial airline pilot for a major US airline. I currently am a Captain on the Boeing 737. I am type rated and experienced on the Boeing 767, 757, and the Airbus A320. I also have experience as a Captain on several other aircraft, namely, the Lockheed Electra L-188 (a civilian version of the P-3 Orion), the Convair 580, plus numerous others. My journey into this industry has been an interesting one. That could be a whole book by itself, but I will give a summary here so you understand how I came to be where I am today.

My life-of-flight expedition began when I was 15 years old as a sophomore in high school. The school guidance counselor at the time asked me to choose physics or chemistry for my science elective. Apparently this was one of many crossroads where I had to choose, to turn left or right. And, of course, don't look back.

It was a time when I seriously had to think about taking a life direction. What was I going to do with my life? I had good grades, attended honors classes, and I was very active. I took part in cheerleading, dancing, competitive diving, martial arts, student council, and a variety of other social and education-based activities. But like most teenagers, my life didn't yet have direction or a plan.

Turn left or right? Here was the question in front of me, Chemistry or Physics? I told my counselor I didn't want to waste time on classes that would not benefit me in some future career. I almost hear him thinking "Come on Laura, Chemistry or Physics – I've got twenty more students to talk to."

Clearly I had to think about what I wanted. I wanted to travel. I wanted to meet different people, work in the outdoors. I wanted to see things. I wanted to help people, feel like I made a difference, and (oh yeah) be able to pay my bills while doing all that.

A list of careers that fit some of my criteria included Park Ranger, Cruise Ship Director, Recreational Resort Leader, and Flight Attendant. Well, they were interesting, but they did not seem very challenging academically. Being very strong in math and science, I needed something more. Still frustrated by the inability to decide anything, I shelved it. Fortunately for my future, I chose Physics.

Later that week, a friend read my list and zeroed in on the last one, Flight Attendant. "What about being the pilot?" she suggested. I marveled at how cool the idea of that sounded. A pilot, yes, I could do that!

I immediately contacted my counselor with my newly found destiny. I have to admit, I was concerned at first because I had never seen or heard of a woman pilot before, so I wasn't sure if the airlines or military would let me fly airplanes. After being assured that it was possible, I set out to get as much information as I could on how to become a pilot.

Telling my parents about my idea was a bit of a challenge. They were divorced, so I had to break the news to each of them individually. I called my dad first, explaining to him in a very excited voice what I had chosen to do. His initial response was a bit underwhelming. "That would be great, but not many women fly," he said. He had what some people call a bit of Old School thinking.

Next, I told my mom. Her response was equally underwhelming. "It's too dangerous," she said. Plus she added it was too expensive to learn to fly, and she could not afford to help pay for it. Besides, she thought it was probably just a phase I was going through. She even said, "You'll get over it."

Up in the Air

"Great. I guess I'm on my own with this," I recall thinking. Fortunately, my mom had a co-worker who owned a plane. She told him about her daughter's newly found passion, and Mr. Sevelle offered to take me up for a flight. I was ecstatic! Up we went soon after. I was instantly hooked! Now I was determined to make this my life. I worked three jobs to pay for my flying lessons. Whatever it took, I would do it.

My first solo flight came, ironically, right after I got my driver's license. I continued to work my way through the levels of flying experience, solo-ing on my 16th birthday and receiving my private pilot license shortly after turning 17 years old (the legal age). For college, I decided that I wanted to go to the best aviation school in order to achieve my goal of becoming a pilot for one of the major airlines. I applied to the United States Air Force Academy and received a Congressional nomination.

Shortly before the academy made their final decisions, I contacted the Air Force recruiter to ask if they could guarantee that I would be given the chance to go to flight training once I graduated. The answer was "No." The pilot slots were very competitive, and there were no guarantees that I could attend Air Force pilot training.

A critical decision was facing me. Do I go to a school that might or might not allow me to become a pilot, or do I do it on my own? It was a difficult question, but I realized that I had to stay in control of my own destiny. I reluctantly removed myself from consideration for the Academy and looked for another path to my goal.

At this point, I was completely on my own. Problems at home had pushed me out into the world sooner than most. I had no money for college, and wishing to become a pilot wasn't enough. I started to work a few side jobs to pay the bills. Anything left over went to food and flying lessons. When there wasn't enough, I ate less and flew more.

Slowly I got more and more flight experience. Following a few months of this, I was able to attend a local community college and begin to get the pre-requisite classes accomplished. I desperately wanted to go to a premier aviation school, but I wasn't sure how I'd pay for the education even if I were lucky enough to get accepted.

Takeoff Roll

Finally, my big break came when a university in Florida called Embry-Riddle Aeronautical University called to offer me admission to their Aeronautical Science Pilot program. Along with the admission came a financial aid plan that helped to cover the costs of my classes. Upon hearing about the acceptance letter, my grandmother offered to help pay for some of my living expenses as well. She called my dad and got him to commit to help financially when he could. And much to my surprise, my other grandmother chipped in, too!

After years of hoping and wishing, I finally had the means to make it work. Off I went to ERAU – the self-proclaimed "Harvard of the Skies." To make a really long story short, I worked extremely hard at my education and the rest of my flight certifications. I completed my education at Embry-Riddle in 2 ½ years, hands-down the happiest graduate in my class!

I was invited to come back to teach flying as an instructor at ERAU, but I chose to return to California instead. I took a job as a flight instructor for Trade Winds Aviation in San Jose, CA. I was ecstatic to actually be getting paid to fly and to teach what I loved. My students were amazing, so I really enjoyed what I was doing. I loved guiding them and watching them get excited about flying.

Years later, I was hired by an airline named Renown. Ironically, this company flew military contracts as well as civilian charters. Having turned down the military path to becoming a pilot, here I was flying Navy personnel back and forth between the various bases in southern California. I flew first as a copilot on the Convair 580 (a 60,000 lb, large

50 passenger, two-engine aircraft) and quickly upgraded to Captain. We flew charters for sports teams, movie production companies, casino runs – you name it, we flew it.

Every flight was a new adventure. I loved the challenges, the crews, the passengers. Soon, I upgraded from the Convair to an L-188 Lockheed Electra (a 130,000 lb, 100-passenger, four-engine civilian P3 aircraft). This brought about a whole new chapter of flying for me. I started also flying cargo internationally between Germany and Ireland.

On top of all this flying, I was doing the air show circuit in my downtime with my close friend, Wanda Collins. As the Director of Operations, I was responsible for the logistics, planning, marketing, and support of her air show performances, while I practiced aerobatic flying as well.

High Performance

Every six months, I applied to the major airlines, with the hope that somebody would notice my resume. I was especially intrigued with one airline in particular. I loved their image, professionalism, route structures, pilot bases, airplanes, hiring philosophies, everything. I did all that was humanly possible to get an interview with them. It became my job to convince them that I had what they needed.

Finally, I got a call one day to come for an interview. I ran the gauntlet of trials to get onboard – a grueling panel interview, simulator tests, a thorough medical exam, followed by an aggressive down-select of candidates. Twelve of us started the process as candidates for the airline that day. In the end, they chose two, which was about the standard ratio for making the cut. Gratefully, I was one of them!

Still thrilled by getting hired for my dream job, right into the throes of training I went. Months of intense ground school, simulator training, emergency procedures, and safety scenarios were now my life. Upon clearing all of these hurdles, I got assigned to a First Officer position on the Boeing 737.

They put me on one year of probationary status, as they do for all new-hire pilots. The message was clear, "Don't screw up at all, or you're fired." I had to bring my 'A' game with everything: my appearance, my conversations, my knowledge, my flying ability. I had to show them that I could continually make the grade.

Life and Love

Despite the challenges of being a new hire, I was set. I had made it! In due time, I made it off probationary status. I married a great man whom I had met back when I started flying before college (another story in itself). He was finishing his stint as a US Air Force Electronic Warfare Officer on the B-52 and transitioning to work as a test engineer for an aircraft manufacturer in Seattle. To my delight after years of training, I was flying the big jets. This was finally the good life, as I had dreamed.

A few years into the dream come true, the darkest day happened. The events of September 11th literally rocked our world. The aviation industry fell into peril. All of the things that we subsequently experienced, both as pilots and as family of pilots, would take another entire book to describe.

The effects from the terrorist attacks rippled through the airlines like aftershocks to a major earthquake. One by one, the carriers fell into financial distress. Some shut down, while some went into bankruptcy. Mine was one of them. Eventually, I was furloughed, so I had to spend my time waiting and watching for a recovery, planning to get re-hired someday. I knew it would happen eventually; I just didn't know how long it might take.

For years, I flipped houses, dabbled in financial advising, and had two precious children, a son and a daughter. Believing in my life as a pilot was a real struggle, but eventually I was asked to return to the cockpit. Just as I resumed piloting, my 2-year-old son became critically ill. I immediately returned home for what was to be the toughest three and a half years of my life. Most of the details of these years will be in my next book, *Lost and Found*. I share some of my accumulated knowledge from that period in the Travel Health section of this book.

Back to You

I have since returned to flying jets, determined more than ever to help you be empowered in your travels and your health. Because of my love for flying, years of experience, knowledge of health, and because I am a caring person, I bring you this book. My mission is to help you overcome your fears. I want you to feel safe and secure when you fly, while building your knowledge base and confidence in the flying experience. Combined with some tips for healthy traveling, you should be able to have that relaxing trip in the skies that we have come to expect.

History

Orville and Wilbur Wright were the first to officially accomplish heavier-than-air sustained flight. Their aircraft, the *Wright Flyer*, was successful mainly due to the unique flight controls it incorporated. The Wright Brothers were the first to design a 3-axis flight control system, allowing independent steering for pitch, roll, and yaw. This steering made it possible to keep a fixed wing aircraft aloft.

December 17th, 1903 was the first sustained flight, a significant milestone in the design of aircraft. So many contributions have occurred since that first flight at Kitty Hawk, NC. These new flying machines were used in photography everywhere, then soon became the weapons of various military applications.

Following World War 1, former military pilots became the barnstormers, performing stunts to show off their flying skills. Air races and air shows were the events to see. The public was enamored with these daring young men. Some of the wealthy bought their way into getting joyrides on these aircraft, beginning a trend of passengers paying for rides on aircraft.

The competition in speed and distance racing demanded better technology. The Golden Age of aviation brought us the transformation from biplanes made of wood and fabric to single wing planes made out of aluminum. Along the way, the engines were made more powerful and piston engine technology matured, allowing higher speeds and better performance.

Pilots, Planes, and Possibilities

Pilots pushed themselves, and with new aircraft capabilities, ocean crossings became possible. Charles Lindbergh was the first pilot to fly solo across the Atlantic Ocean in 1927 in the *Spirit of St Louis*. Meanwhile, Charles Kingsford Smith and his crew were the first to cross the Pacific Ocean in June 1928 in the *Southern Cross*.

Early flights on the Ford Tri-Motor, known as the "Tin Goose," seated only 13 people at a time, eventually converting to 17 people. They flew very low and slow, typically below 16,000 ft, with few of the creature comforts we take for granted today. There was no air conditioning to speak of. The engines were very noisy, and the aircraft structure vibrated constantly. The interior cabin smelled of oil, leather, and disinfectant. Passengers were airsick often, with no one to help them.

The Boeing 80 finally incorporated forced air for passenger comfort, but the turbulence at these lower altitudes was tough on passengers, with their susceptibility to airsickness. To encourage these brave passengers to travel again, airline owners placed small-framed men in the cabins to help load luggage and assuage the concerns of passengers during flight. When airline carrier Pan American started flying to overseas destinations, they hired men for the passenger first aid and emergency procedures associated with these longer overwater flights. These were the first real stewards of the air. Eventually, women were introduced to fill this role as well. Shortly thereafter, the use of women as stewardesses became increasingly popular with travelers.

Business Loves Flying

At the time, only the wealthy and elite could afford to fly. Travel by airplane was much more expensive than the traditional trip by train. People flew mostly out of necessity, not for pleasure. Aviation historian Roger Bilsten said that in the 1930s, "85% of the passengers came from major businesses and high income residential areas."

As the mid 1930's approached and more reliable aircraft like the DC-3, with its more comfortable, less noisy cabin emerged, more of the general public began to fly. In the year 1930, it is estimated that 474,000 passengers flew in commercial aircraft. In 1937, that number increased to just over 1.1 million. Then in the five years that followed, air travel increased by 600%.

In the 1940s, the aviation industry's attention was diverted to provide military aircraft to support World War II. The technological advances made to meet the needs of the war would soon spill over to commercial transportation. A surplus of military aircraft and production capacity, combined with an increased demand for passenger travel, led to even better commercial aircraft. The manufacture of long-range bombers gave the industry a foundation of high-altitude, extended distance passenger aircraft. In 1946, the first scheduled passenger flight flew out of Heathrow airport in London on an Avro Lancastrian, a converted bomber.

The first production commercial jetliner flew in July 1949, a deHavilland DH 106 Comet. USSR's Aeroflot airline was the first to fly regularly scheduled flights in September 1956, with the Tupolev Tu-104. Boeing created the 707 in late 1957 and brought the Jet Age to aviation. This was the beginning of real safety and comfort for passengers on a large scale.

Beyond Cool

US Air Force Captain Chuck Yeager broke the sound barrier in 1947 in the rocket-powered Bell aircraft. Of course, I cannot write this chapter without mentioning the incredible engineering feat by engineer

Kelly Johnson of Lockheed Skunk Works in the development of the SR-71 Blackbird. This work of art was created well before its time from scratch. The Blackbird could fly at Mach 3 and reach altitudes of 80,000ft. This beauty was a spy plane built after the U-2 to fly above radar tracking and out fly any missiles deployed against it.

Neil Armstrong and Buzz Aldrin stepped onto the surface of the moon and explored it, with Michael Collins overseeing from the command module of Apollo 11 in July 1969. The same year, Boeing introduced the largest passenger jet, the 747. Aerospatiale then created the supersonic passenger jet called Concorde. In the 1980s, an amazing crew of Dick Rutan and Jeanna Yeager flew around the world in Voyager, staying aloft the entire time without stopping for fuel. Pilots were continuing to push themselves and their flying craft to new heights of performance in the wild blue yonder.

Entering a new relationship with space flight, we watched as the first Space Shuttle Orbiter Columbia launched into space, then re-entered the atmosphere and landed on a long runway, looking just as if it was a jetliner. Not quite the same, though; shuttle pilots must approach the runway at a 17-19 degree nose-down descent angle, compared to a typical 3 degree approach for an airliner. They only have one shot to get it right, since there is no going around for a second approach. Compared to a gently gliding jetliner, landing the shuttle has been described as "like landing a brick."

How Far We've Come

Jim Brewer, an aviation enthusiast and frequent traveler who built scores of aircraft models and collected posters from aircraft manufacturers, recalls:

> "My oldest traceable ancestor was John Brewer, an officer on Sir Francis Drake's ship, the Golden Hind. In those days a voyage might take two years. Later forebears came out the Oregon Trail from Manhattan, Kansas by covered wagon and horseback, and it took them five months. During President Grant's time (mid- to late 1800s), a famous Indian fighter and messenger used train, stage coach, and horseback from Washington DC to the California/Oregon border, and it took about 3 weeks. Now with the miracle of air travel, it only takes about five and a half hours! We scarcely appreciate the amazing flight age we are living in when just about anyone can make this trip."

During the 70s and 80s, commercial flying began shifting from passengers of the upper class and royalty toward the general public, in a more mass-transit mode of operation. The ticket price for the first Pan Am flight on a Boeing 707 in 1958 - from New York to London with a stopover in Newfoundland - cost $272 dollars in coach. In 1972, it cost $200 to fly from Los Angeles to Minneapolis.

As I write this today in 2014, I can find flights that cost nearly the same as in 1972. Now, <u>that</u> is a privilege! Prices of most other industry products and services increase with inflation over time. But due to efficiencies in the industry, the price of airline travel has remained steady for over half a century.

The Jets

I continue to marvel at the awesomeness of these jet liners. The structural integrity is unparalleled. From the earliest stages, the aircraft is designed and engineered to precise specifications, or "spec," as it's called. World-class teams of professionals pore over every detail to determine how the design meets the specs of airline regulators such as the Federal Aviation Administration (FAA), the customer airline, the airline market, and the company's own technical criteria. Several different departments within the manufacturing company oversee the project. The design is then reviewed for the go-ahead, but not until every question has been answered, every stone has been turned, and every challenge is addressed.

Design for Performance

In the design phase, exact miniature model replicas of these jet designs are put through extensive testing in giant wind tunnels. This allows the engineers to study how the design might actually perform in-flight. They also use extensive computer modeling which allows them to manipulate millions of environmental parameters to see how they affect the design. After months of testing, the data is analyzed and the best overall design is chosen so that full-scale production can begin.

Once the design is finalized, every component begins production under companies around the world with specific expertise in their respective areas. Engines are meticulously designed and tested, structure is manufactured with laser-guided accuracy, systems are designed and interfaced over and over. It is truly a ballet of thousands of ingenious designs, each independently impressive.

Each part then comes together in sub-assembly plants, and those sub-assemblies eventually come to a final assembly plant where the actual aircraft will be built. Here at the final assembly plant, the mechanics, line workers, and engineers work together to assure that exceptional quality standards are met as they create these beautiful flying machines. All assemblies are checked multiple times to ensure the reliability of the final product.

Testing 1

After several units of the new aircraft are built, it goes immediately into a rigorous series of tests. One unit goes into a large rig for static (motionless) testing. Here, loads are systematically applied similar to and even beyond anything the aircraft will ever experience in flight. Thousands of sensors monitor the stresses in the structure to ensure they are at or below those calculated by the engineers. One of the more infamous tests is the load testing of the wings. Here the wings are flexed up to their maximum design load, and in some instances, up to their ultimate load (the point at which the load should permanently damage the structure).

Just so that you are aware, the design load defines the limits that we pilots stay within. We never go near them, much less beyond them. Even so, the ultimate load is significantly above the design load (typically 50% above).

Here's something else to give you comfort. When Boeing did the static test on the B777 airframe, they expected the wing to fail at its ultimate load of 153% of the design load. It didn't. They had to keep applying more and more load to get the wing to break. It finally did, at 160% of design load, a full 7% above the analysis!

What does this mean to you as the passenger? In anything but the most extreme situations, the airplane structure isn't going to just break. In the case of commercial aircraft wings, you could put an entire professional football team on top of the wings, and they would not break.

Testing 2

Another early unit of the new aircraft goes into a dynamic rig for fatigue testing. Here the structure is subjected to thousands of cycles. And by cycles, I mean everything that the airplane would experience on a typical flight profile: takeoff, cruise, and landing (that's one cycle). This includes pressurization and depressurization of the cabin, flexing the wings, raising and lowering landing gear, and repeated bending & twisting of the fuselage.

Think of bending a wire coat hanger back and forth, over and over until the metal eventually snaps. That's fatigue. The manufacturer needs to show that even after two to three lifetimes of cycles (more than any airplane would ever experience), the airplane structure will not fail due to fatigue.

I know it can be somewhat disconcerting as you fly along to see the wings flexing in-flight. Just realize that the jets are designed this way intentionally. If the structure did not flex, it would be much more prone to fatigue and failure.

The best comparisons I can give you are skyscrapers in an earthquake. The old, rigid stone buildings tend to crack, crumble, and even fall. Newer buildings are designed to flex and sway slightly with the motion of the quake, and so the energy goes into flexing, not breaking the structure.

It is the same with aircraft. Think of the flexing as the aircraft absorbing and safely dissipating the disturbance from turbulence or a firm landing. And by the way, every commercial airliner must demonstrate that it can naturally dampen out these flexing motions, and relatively quickly.

Ok, but what about the new "plastic" composite airplanes? These technologies are also very safe. The military has been using most of these aircraft composites in fighter aircraft that can withstand maneuvers which impose over 9 times the force of gravity (9 Gs) on their structures. Many of these jets can fly faster than twice the speed of sound (Mach 2 or over 1500 mph), and can sustain battle damage from enemy fire while still flying just fine. They will be very durable for your flight from New York to Los Angeles at 1 G and 500 mph.

Testing 3

When Boeing developed its latest 787 aircraft, they addressed this question in a unique way. They manufactured a piece of the fuselage structure and mounted it on a portable stand. They gave each customer – prospective pilots, engineers, and airline executives alike - a turn to strike the structure with a sledgehammer. They couldn't damage it. They left satisfied.

The manufacturer then places one or more of the first production units into a flight test program (the 787 test program consisted of six test aircraft). Here, the aircraft need to demonstrate compliance with hundreds of FAA and other regulatory requirements to show they are safe for commercial use. They have to show acceptable performance in the most extreme situations: significant turbulence, severe icing, maximum braking, maximum crosswinds, and the like. So take comfort - no matter how bad the conditions, the airplane has flown in much worse during certification testing, and it did just fine.

The Magic of Physics

Let's talk about how the jets actually fly. If you look at an aircraft sitting on the ground, you will see that the forward leading edge of the wing is slightly higher than the back part of the wing (i.e., the wing is tilted up). This means that the wing has a positive tilt angle, called its angle of incidence.

The wing also has camber, which is its curvature. If you took a cross-sectional cut of the wing, it would look like a warped, elongated teardrop. Yes, like a woman's body, it is svelte, smooth, and curved.

As the engines produce thrust, the aircraft moves forward and air begins to flow over and under the wing surface. Those unique curves on the wing make the airflow on top of the wings go faster than the airflow on the bottom of the wings. In the layer of airflow closest to the wing surface, called the boundary layer, the magic of physics happens. The faster boundary layer airflow on top of the wing creates a lower pressure than on the bottom (aka the Bernoulli Principle). The faster the airplane goes, the greater this pressure difference, the greater lift on the wing, until ultimately the airplane is lifted in to the sky.

We can increase this lifting effect by changing the curves on the wing. On large aircraft, we do this using forward edge slats and trailing edge flaps. The more curved the wing, the more lifting we get. We use this for more efficient lift on takeoff, so we don't need as much runway to get off the ground. We also use these trailing edge flaps and our landing gear to create more of an angle and drag during landings.

Engine Power

The thrust power from just one jet engine is incredibly strong. On my 250-passenger Boeing 767, the thrust can be as high as 60,000 lbs per engine (about 24,000 horsepower each). On a Boeing 777, it can be as high as 115,000 lbs!

The main engine manufacturers on large commercial aircraft are General Electric, Pratt & Whitney, and Rolls Royce. They are extremely reliable, quiet, and fuel-efficient. Strides are being made to make them even more ecological, including the use of new bio-fuels and the development of hybrid engines that can go under electrical power during cruise. There was a study done that showed a significant reversal of ozone depletion for the days that followed Sept 11th, when all aviation flights were grounded.

On twin-engine airliners, the engines are certified to allow the jet to completely lose all thrust on one engine and still fly a fully loaded aircraft to safety. Even if the engine failure occurred on takeoff, the one good engine has the capability to lift the aircraft off the ground, clear obstacles (mountains, etc.), and climb to a safe altitude.

Engine manufacturers put the engines through extensive testing to meet even the most severe challenges. For example, while operating on a test stand at their facility, they will force large quantities of water, huge chunks of ice, and even dead bird carcasses into the engine inlets to make sure they keep operating.

Engines are designed to withstand the worst conditions imaginable in flight. They are very reliable. Currently, if engines are maintained properly per the manufacturer's guidelines, the probability of a structural failure in an engine is 1 in 100 million - now that's safety!

Doing Without

In the remote chance that all engines quit, a jetliner simply becomes a big glider. As long as we keep the airflow over the wings and a safe speed, the aircraft will not stall. Simply put, the aircraft will not fall out of the sky.

In glide conditions, some airplanes would kick out a small device called a RAT, or ram air turbine. This is kind of a small windmill. The wind turns the RAT propeller blades, generating enough electricity to power the flight controls and other critical systems on the airplane.

As a pilot rule-of-thumb, we can glide at a 3 to 1 ratio. What I mean by that is for every 1000 feet we descend in altitude, we move forward 3 nautical miles toward the nearest suitable airport. So from 40,000ft, we have a glide range of about 120 nautical miles. This gliding capability is one of the reasons that the amazing US Air pilots on Flight 1549 were able to make it over to the Hudson River for an emergency water landing.

Layers of Protection

The jet systems are designed to have no single points of failure. In other words, there are redundancies to back up each system if it fails. If an airspeed indicator fails, there is a backup.

In some cases, there are triple redundancies on critical systems to protect the crew and passengers. One example is the flight computers that analyze all of the airspeed, altitude, and other critical information. There are three of them, and they always talk to each other, comparing data. If one goes astray, the other two take over and the faulty computer shuts itself down.

The probability of failure for any system or group of systems is heavily regulated by the FAA and foreign regulatory agencies. So take comfort in knowing that every airplane system has repeatedly demonstrated the required reliability.

Deferral Safety

There is a standard protocol where the manufacturer, the FAA, and the airline maintenance department can allow the repair of a system or a portion of a system to be deferred. This means it can be fixed at a later time or location. Ultimately, it is our decision as your pilots to decide whether we think it is safe enough to fly the flight once we weigh all of the factors involved. We work for you, the passenger, when we look at all the options.

Many of us ask ourselves if we would take the jet if our family were onboard. We know each and every one of you are important in this world, and we take that very seriously. Please do not get angry if we cancel a flight and inconvenience you due to a maintenance issue. We may be literally saving your life that day with our decisions.

Your Flying Lesson for the Day

We have various flight control systems that work together for us to effectively operate the aircraft. The primary flight controls are the ailerons, rudders, and elevators. The ailerons are on the back edges of the wings and help us roll the airplane so we can turn.

Remember how the lift on the wing works? Well, as we move the control yoke or stick to the right, the ailerons on the right wing deflect upward. This causes the airflow to force the right wing downward. At the same time, the ailerons on the left wing deflect downward, causing more curve on the wing and thus more lift, which forces the left wing upward. As a result, we begin to turn the jet to the right.

The rudder is located on the back edge of the vertical tail. We control this with our foot pedals. If we step on the right foot pedal, the rudder will deflect to the right and into the airstream, making drag and pushing the tail. This makes the nose of the jet go to right, rotating around the vertical axis.

The elevators are located on the back edge of the horizontal part of the tail. When we pull the control yoke or stick back towards us, the elevators deflect upward and into the airstream, which creates drag on top of the horizontal portion of the tail and pushed it downward. When the tail goes downward, the nose rises. With a little added thrust, this allows us to climb.

Our secondary flight controls consist of speed brakes, spoilers (panels on top of the wing that assist with roll control), landing gear (tires and brakes), antiskid systems for the brakes, an automatic braking system, and backup flight control systems.

Electrical Works

The electrical system is supported by external power while the aircraft is on the ground. It consists of generators, an auxiliary power unit (APU), electrical buses, and transformer rectifiers. The generators have constant speed drives that are run off of the engines. The APU is actually a very small jet engine located in the back of the tail. It acts as both an electric generator and air pump for the cabin cooling system.

These electrical system components are redundant to each other and can transfer electric loads to other sources if one of the components fails. The aircraft will shed some of its non-essential electrical draws if it needs to support its main systems better. Just like in your home, we have circuit breakers and push buttons that allow us to reset a system that may have tripped offline for some reason.

If all electricity quits, we have batteries as backups for approximately 30 minutes. The engines, flight controls, and some basic flight instruments will still run so that we can get safely on the ground. Over-water aircraft have the RAT generator, which I discussed previously.

Cloud-Busting

Many times I am asked how we fly in the clouds. Almost all aircraft have an instrument called an attitude indicator that provides the pilots an artificial horizon by which to fly. It actually simulates the sky, the aircraft, and the ground on a gage. We rely on this instrument for horizon information in relation to pitch and bank angles while in clouds or when the actual horizon is not visible.

We also have indicators for airspeed, altitude, vertical speed, turn & slip, horizontal situation, and engine controls. The fancier jets have moving maps, weather radar, etc. Much of this information is combined on a few flat screen displays.

Most of us pilots, no matter what type of airplanes we flew for our initial pilot training, were taught "pitch and power," meaning that you can fly any aircraft if you know the pitch settings (where to put the nose of the aircraft, for example 2 degrees above the horizon) and what power setting to use (such as engine pressure ratio, EPR or N1) for your desired state of flight.

Another foundation pilot lesson is that "airspeed is life," meaning no matter what the situation, you always keep airflow over the wings. Pastor Joyce Meyer has used the attitude indicator as an analogy for a good life. She said, "If you keep your nose up, above the horizon, with a positive attitude, you will climb upward. If your nose is down with a negative attitude, you will go down."

Fuel Flow

The fuel system is the heart of an aircraft. Much like the blood in our bodies, we need this fuel pumping and circulating throughout the aircraft without any artery clogging issues. Clean and lean jet fuel is loaded into the aircraft from the fuel trucks at a specific access point on the wing. Most jets have their fuel tanks in the wings, which helps structural integrity and stability, while some larger jets have additional tanks in the center portion of the aircraft. A new Boeing 747-8 Intercontinental can carry as much as 64,055 gallons of fuel, that's over 200 tons of fuel!

Just like your car, the heavier the airplane is, and the faster you go, the more fuel you will burn. For planning purposes, we know what the optimal altitudes and speeds are for fuel efficiency. These depend on the atmospheric condition, route, direction, winds, weight, etc. for the planned flight.

It is ultimately up to us, the pilots to determine how much fuel we think we need for the flight, considering all of the factors. There is a term we call "bingo" fuel, which is our determined minimum fuel amount. If we reach the bingo fuel minimum, this means no more messing around in holding, vectors, deviations, etc. We need to get on the ground now.

We can tell Air Traffic Control as a pre-emptive measure that we are "minimum fuel," but when we say we are "emergency fuel," this means we are now first priority to land. In terms of time, this is usually around 30 minutes of fuel remaining.

Nice Cool Air

The pressurization and air conditioning system uses a combination of outside air (collected by a big scoop on the bottom of the jet), and compressed, filtered hot air. We regulate the pressure inside the cabin by using an automatic system that opens and closes an outflow valve. On the ground, the outflow valve is fully opened, depressurizing the aircraft.

As we take off, the valve will close, allowing the jet to pressurize to the desired cabin pressure of 8.6 PSI (pounds per square inch), equivalent to around 8,000 ft of altitude. Once this is reached, the system will vary the amount the valve is open in order to maintain this setting. The rate at which this pressurization happens is 300 ft per minute on climb out and depressurization of 500 ft per minute on descent.

Some aircraft perform the pressurization function better than others. This is why you may feel the pressure in your ears during some flights and not on others. Some of this is the pressurization system itself, and some of it is due to the air seals around the various doors and windows. Just as with cars, the seals around the doors and windows are not as effective over time, so air can leak on older aircraft, making it harder for the pressurization system to keep up. For redundancy, there is a second, standby automatic pressurization system and a backup manual system.

If a rapid depressurization happened, this would probably be from an outflow valve opening fully. It is unlikely that a rapid depressurization would ever occur due a small hole, which was initially a concern of passengers when Federal Air Marshals were deployed onto commercial airliners. There was a fear that a hole the size of a bullet could breach the cabin and cause a sudden depressurization. However, leaks from small holes or leaky seals would actually create a slow leak, allowing us time to descend gradually and divert. There have been situations in the past when aircraft have had large holes such as cargo doors that were inadvertently left unlatched and the aircraft was still able to fly, albeit unpressurized.

Safer In Than Out

Pressurization is the reason you don't need to worry about someone opening a cabin door or escape window in flight. All Boeing aircraft doors and windows open inward. This means the cabin pressure is holding the door shut with such force that no human can possibly overcome it in fight.

How much force? Well, if you do the rough math, the difference in pressure between the cabin and the outside air at 39,000 ft is around 8 lbs per square inch. A typical 737 cabin entry door measures 34" x 72". That means the area of the door is 2,448 square inches. Multiply 8 lbs/sq inch x 2,448 sq inches = 19,584 lbs.

So unless you know someone who can pull a 10 Ton sled across the yard, relax. Nobody can open the door in flight. Oh, and the escape windows are about 20" x 38" = 760 sq inches. So it takes 6,080 lbs of force to open those in flight. I don't know anyone who has a 3-ton pull capability either.

Cozy and Comfortable

For temperature control, cold outside ram air is mixed with hot compressed air and put through air cycle machines, then fine-tuned with trim air valves for precise temperatures. There are different zones in the aircraft, allowing for better temperature regulation in the different passenger areas. The newer commercial jets allow the flight attendants to control the temperatures using independent controllers located in each zone. The older jets have the selectors in the cockpit so we must rely on the gages and communication from the passengers and flight attendants as to the comfort in their respective zones.

As part of recent changes, most airlines no longer offer pillows or blankets. They have been removed from the aircraft in order to cut costs and save weight. When you travel, be sure to layer your clothing so you don't get too hot or cold. And if you do get hot or cold, speak up! There may be something we can do about it.

Other Controls

The hydraulic systems are very comprehensive. Most of the time on a twin-engine jet, there are three systems. Again, there is safety in the redundancy. Each system has specific items to which it provides hydraulic power.

The systems can, however, work in conjunction with one another if needed. For example, if there were a leak in the left system, the right system can provide hydraulic power and sometimes fluid to critical aircraft items such as flight controls, landing gear, and flaps. Other components that use hydraulics are brakes, nose wheel steering, and several smaller actuators throughout the airplane.

Even without any hydraulic power, most aircraft can be controlled using manual backups. Landing gear can be lowered mechanically by gravity. In the case of United Airlines flight 232 in Sioux City, Iowa, the heroic pilots were able to steer the aircraft by using engine thrust, having no hydraulics at all. They got the airplane onto the runway and saved 185 lives.

What Was That Sound?

Aircraft sounds can be unnerving for people who are not used to them. Once you are onboard the airplane, you will hear many operational sounds from both the jet and the crew. The airflow through the cabin vents will create a "whoosh" sound as increasing amounts of air are pushed through the cabin. Usually, this is most noticeable when we go from no airflow or airflow from a ground cart to our APU air.

Sometimes if you are sitting toward the back of the cabin, you can actually hear the APU slowly spinning up. It sounds just like a miniature jet engine starting, because, well, that's what it is. Once the APU power is selected, you will likely hear a high-pitched constant hum.

You may also hear a high-pitched squeal from the bottom of the plane. Typically this is just the cargo door hydraulic pump operating; it should stop once the cargo doors are closed and latched. If you sit near the windows, aft of the wings, you can sometimes see the open cargo doors and the ramp personnel loading your luggage.

On the Airbus A319/A320, you may hear what sounds like a "barking dog." This is an electrical hydraulic pump that senses the pressure differential between the different hydraulic systems and then "pumps up" the low system – sounds like "ruff!" Then there are smaller ruffs as the pressure bleeds down. Oh yes, and sometimes you may actually hear a real dog bark. If someone brought a dog along for the flight, the dog is down in the pressurized and temperature controlled cargo area.

Pilots

We pilots usually start our journey in this profession by being sparked with the intriguing idea of flying airplanes. Then, once we try it, we are addicted.

Studies have shown that most of us are cut from the same cloth when it comes to personality and thinking styles. We tend to think in absolutes, black and white, structured. We are mission-oriented task masters who are continually forward thinking. We are intelligent and very effective at compartmentalizing. We are technically proficient and have strong eye-hand coordination. We tend to be problem solvers who take into account various facts and detail in order to make our decisions. We are determined, driven, disciplined, and organized.

We usually are considered to have Type A personalities and want to have control of everything we can. We are safety-minded and tend to be conservative in our thoughts and actions. We usually keep emotions to a minimum, and may appear at times to come off as arrogant. But control of emotions is just another form of control to us.

Emotions And Expectations

One emotion we feel comfortable displaying to the public is confidence. This is likely because we know that is what the public needs from us and expects from us. And we tend to set that expectation for ourselves.

In fact, we set very high expectations for ourselves, for our fellow pilots, and for others in general. We trust each other implicitly in the cockpit and assume that other pilots are trustworthy as well. While these personality traits allow us to be the best at what we do, it can be a challenge for our spouses, family, and friends if we are not understood for who we are.

Pilot Careers

Once we decide that we want to become pilots, we embark on a journey through research. There are various pilot career options such as airline, military, cargo, corporate, regional carrier, test pilot, astronaut, rescue pilot, bush pilot, medical services pilot, law enforcement pilot, tour pilot, news pilot, float plane pilot, and instructor pilot. Basically if there is a need to transport someone or something via the airways, you can find a career as a pilot.

There are two general paths that the typical pilot can take in order to accomplish the goal of a pilot career. Primarily it consists of either training in the military programs or training as a civilian. The path is long and arduous, marked by levels of proficiency, similar to the kind of training that doctors undergo in order to achieve the right to practice medicine.

First, we must persevere through extensive schooling and higher education in basic subjects as well as aviation trade-specific classes. In most flying careers, a college education and degree is required for employment.

Just like the aspiring doctor takes anatomy 101 to learn about the human body and how its systems work, we pilots take extensive ground school classes to learn not just how our airplane works, but how everything else works as well. We learn how the weather works, we learn how the air traffic control system works, we learn about airports and how they operate, we learn about government regulation for conducting flights, navigation, and we learn real quick that this pilot thing is way more than how well you can fly an airplane.

Reliable Responses

Whether it be through military or civilian training, the pilots need to ingrain emergency procedures, aircraft systems, flight regulations, and a host of other items so that they become second nature, almost instinctual. Some of this is done before we ever set foot on an airplane and some is done in parallel to the flight training. The flight training starts with learning basic flying, then you work your way up various levels of skill, achievement, and experience. Each certification, or phase completion, builds on the one before.

In each stage, we are required to study extensively, attend ground training classes, and pass knowledge tests. Then we step into the simulators and the training aircraft to work with instructors who help teach us about the airplane, its characteristics, and the training requirements of that particular rating, certification, or phase.

Now, in addition to learning the basics of aviation and the skills required to pass each rating, pilots must be uniquely checked out in the aircraft they are operating. Aircraft are all different in their designs and performance. So the pilot must be very familiar with how to operate that aircraft effectively and safely.

Not Quite Like Driving

A good analogy to put this in perspective is getting your driver license for the first time. Typically you start out taking a class and studying the fundamentals. Then, you receive driver's education in a training car with an instructor skilled and experienced in teaching the car's characteristics, performance, and how to operate it. The instructor passes along techniques, rules of thumb, and requirements to you as the student driver. After you've studied, passed a written test on the laws and rules of driving, and demonstrated skill and proficiency in driving, you would be awarded a license to operate a motor vehicle.

Here's where things are a bit different for pilots. Imagine if that license said you can only drive in the daytime, on sunny days, and only in the car you took your test in. That's right, just because you can drive a small sedan, does not mean you are allowed to drive an SUV, or a pickup truck, or a Lamborghini. This is how it is with pilot licenses and ratings. You might have a license, but you can only fly in VFR (visual flight rules) and only in the aircraft that you've shown proficiency in flying.

Let's go back to our analogy. Just like a licensed driver cannot just start driving a city bus, tractor trailer semi, or a piece of construction equipment, a pilot cannot just go get practice flying an aircraft and get checked out. There are special licenses a pilot must attain to operate commercial aircraft.

The pilot must build not just knowledge but also experience in order to effectively operate larger and more complicated aircraft. On average, it takes about 8 years (or about 5,000 flight hours) of continuous dedication in order to achieve the level of proficiency to be a first officer and another 5 years (or another 3,000 flight hours) to be ready to qualify as a captain.

Captain and Copilot

There are two pilots in the flight deck on a commercial aircraft. One is the captain (the one with 4 stripes on the shoulders), who flies from the left seat and has ultimate authority over the aircraft, its crew and the passengers. The other is the first-officer or copilot (the one with 3 stripes on the shoulders) who flies from the right seat, shares the workload, and performs much of the preflight duties.

Both pilots are fully qualified to fly the aircraft. Their experience can vary greatly depending on background (a copilot can sometimes have more total hours than a captain), but the minimum experience of either pilot is typically 5,000 flight hours or about 8 calendar years. That's about the same duration as medical school, and rightfully so. Pilots as well as doctors hold your lives in our hands every day.

Once we have reached the stage of becoming qualified as commercial transport pilots, we continue to grow and gain experience so that as we encounter various situations, we have the background to respond appropriately.

Physical Readiness

There are many requirements that we must continually meet in order to keep our jobs. One such requirement that we must meet every six months is an FAA medical exam. I like to fondly call this 'career roulette.' There aren't too many careers out there that can end instantly by a doctor's exam, but ours is one of them. Our anxiety and blood pressure usually go up just before stepping into the doctor's office. We always wonder if this is the day our career is over and are relieved when the answer is "not yet."

The FAA has very strict medical requirements. This is why you rarely ever hear of a pilot having some sort of medical emergency onboard an airplane. Pilots are also subject to random drug and alcohol testing.

That doesn't mean all pilots are the perfect picture of health. That would be unrealistic. Living up to fifty percent of your life on the road means limited healthy food choices, irregular sleep/wake patterns, and fewer chances to participate in regular exercise. The nature of the job creates health challenges we all must overcome, and the first is dehydration.

Health Maintenance

The cabin and flight deck environment is very dry. The air circulated throughout the cabin has a very low humidity and tends to exacerbate the dehydration caused by not drinking enough water. This can rapidly lead to fatigue as well as health problems.

With the higher security procedures now required to enter and exit the flight deck, pilots have a harder time getting drinks of water from the cabin galleys or having the flight attendants bring them drinks to the flight deck. In fact, after the events of Sept 11th, 2001 there was a noted increase in the number of pilots suffering from kidney stones. It is believed that excessive dehydration may have contributed to this.

Another issue pilots face is the restriction on most over-the-counter medications that the public has access to. Most cold medications, allergy medications, sleep aids, and other meds design to help alleviate symptoms are not allowed for pilots. Anti-depressants, stress relief remedies, and any mood-altering medications are prohibited. Even pilot alcohol consumption, despite the media stereotypes, is closely restricted and monitored by both the FAA and the airline companies.

Time Shifts

Perhaps the largest pilot medical challenge is that of fatigue. Flight schedules can require a pilot to show for an afternoon flight one day, an all-nighter flight the next day, a layover on day 3, then a 5:00am show on day 4. This swing-shifting over a relatively short period of days can profoundly fatigue a pilot.

The human body prefers routine sleep/wake cycles, but pilots don't have that luxury. The FAA requirements as well as pilot union contracts help control some of these scheduling issues, but fatiguing schedules are still flown continuously.

On top of the flying schedule, we deal with the effects of crossing multiple time zones. Despite where the pilot is located, his or her internal body clock is set to the home time zone. Hence, a 5:00am show in New York for someone based out of Los Angeles is actually a 2:00am show to that person's body clock. Fatigue can run the pilot down and increase susceptibility to medical illness or maladies.

It Takes Two

In the rare case that one of the pilots has a medical issue, the other pilot can take over and do what it takes to get the airplane safely to the ground. This is another great example of critical redundancy in this industry. The flight deck used to have a third pilot, the flight engineer, but the advent of computers allowed the monitoring functions of the flight engineer to be automated.

The new requirement is for two pilots on commercial transport. This is a good point for me to make a plea to all of you airline passengers out there. There have been certain airline executives proposing going to a one-pilot flight deck, with a minimally flight qualified crewmember as a backup pilot in the case of an emergency. They see this as a way to save labor expenses. As the flying public, you should demand nothing less than two fully qualified, well-experienced pilots flying your aircraft. And they should be properly and fully trained by rigorous airline training programs.

Always At School

Another factor in piloting is the amount of training and expectations that we must meet. Each year, we do a series of ground school sessions to review aircraft systems, rules and regulations, and operating procedures. We fly several simulator sessions as a crew with an instructor to practice emergency procedures and non-normal circumstances. Examples of these would be engine failures, fires, rapid decompression, hydraulic failures, electrical anomalies, safety breaches, passenger issues, and even terrorist threats. We are then tested on our knowledge, decision-making, flying skills, and ability to work together for successful outcomes. We are required to do this in order to maintain our proficiency so that we are ready to handle whatever challenges may come our way.

In order to keep you safe, we study throughout the year to stay current on new procedures, technologies, and changes. When we learn to fly a new jet, it normally takes 5 weeks of 12-hour days at the airline training centers to get ready for qualification. At the end of the training, we have a fully comprehensive simulator check ride with an FAA check pilot that we must pass in order to be cleared and qualified to fly that model of aircraft.

After the check ride, we go out to the actual airplane for what's called Initial Operating Experience (IOE). We spend several days with an Instructor Pilot flying normal airline operations with passengers onboard. Once the instructor is satisfied, they will sign us off to pilot that model of aircraft on the line. In some cases, when we are qualified as captains, we receive a Type Rating in that specific aircraft.

Training Targets

Unfortunately, there is a lot of economic pressure on airlines to cut labor costs, and flight crew training is one of the many areas that have been targeted. The airline companies have been operating with a relatively inexpensive pilot force since 2001. This was largely due to the pilots taking voluntary pay cuts to help the airline avoid bankruptcy, or help the airline make it through bankruptcy restructuring.

Now that some of the airlines have largely recovered and some pilots are returning (albeit slowly) to normal pay levels, there are initiatives being implemented that continue to reduce pilot training costs. The trend that I'm seeing with our commercial pilot training really concerns me. In some cases, airline training for pilots has been cut back as much as 30% over the past decade. This is a very real and serious concern of the airline pilots and must be addressed.

There is an over-reliance on the fact that the airline safety records have been so exemplary in the United States. The major contributors to this safety record have been the improved technologies in the aircraft and the relatively high level of experience that our current flight crews bring to the cockpit. Newer training programs seem to rely more on the technology built into the airplane and less on the hands-on practice of flying the airplane. Procedures are now being taught online using computer-based lesson modules instead of being practiced in the simulator at company training centers.

Experience Counts

The main reason for the high pilot experience level is because most of us have been frozen in our current aircraft and position since the September 11th attacks. Many airlines have gone out of business or sought bankruptcy protection in the last decade. Other airlines have struggled along or merged with stronger airlines.

With no growth or expansion in the industry, most of us pilots have either stagnated in our current fleet and seat, been downgraded to a lower position due to downsizing, or been furloughed. Most of us have flown the same model aircraft for years, so we know the aircraft extremely well.

In 2007, the mandatory retirement age for pilots was increased from 60 to 65 years old. This is a contributing factor in the ability to retain very experienced pilots in the cockpit over the last 5 years. The safety record stays strong, because despite eroding training, the real-time experience compensates.

At some point, those very experienced pilots will retire, and the majority of us will finally begin moving upward in the pilot ranks. This will restart the need to bring new pilots onboard at airlines across the world. This is when we will start to see the effects of reduced training and procedures being taught on a computer versus practicing them in a full motion simulator.

Who's Flying Whom?

Another aspect about pilot training you should be aware of is the training of pilots for partner airlines and subcontracted regional carriers that fly our routes. These pilots are not trained by the parent airline. You may buy your ticket as a flight on Brand X, but you may notice that one or more of the segments of the trip is operated by a different company.

Regional carriers (such as Brand X "Express" or Brand X "Connections") train and manage their own flight crews. These crews often have less experience than the pilots at the major carriers. This can become a big factor when flying in difficult weather conditions, congested airports, or in mountainous terrain. Just be aware of this when you book your tickets.

Another common practice is code sharing. This is where you book your ticket on major airline Brand X, but major airline Brand Y is the company that operates it. This is a little bit of duping the passenger in my opinion, and it literally is contracting out our jobs to other carriers. I mean, you booked your ticket on Brand X for a reason, so why should you be flying on all these other airlines?

If you want to be flown by the most experienced, skilled, and trained pilots on the safest and most reliable aircraft, then make sure that each segment of your trip is operated by the mainline carrier with whom you booked your ticket.

Safety Protocols and Practices

At the heart of how we operate are checklists, standard operating procedures, and crew coordination. We diligently follow checklists that are put together by the aircraft manufacturer and further enhanced by inputs from the pilots and the airline. Following these ensures that there is a standardized protocol on each and every flight.

We also use Standard Operating Procedures (or SOPs) so that no matter which jet we fly or what crewmembers we work with, the processes and expectations are always the same. We are trained in Crew Resource Management (CRM), which allows us to use all of our available resources to make safe and effective decisions. In unusual circumstances, adherence to these standardized operations become critical and can even save lives.

Checklists, diligently applied, make safety protocols work. There was a medical seminar conducted many years ago with over 200 surgeons in attendance. The speaker had the doctors guess how many medical deaths had occurred due to errors in standard medical procedures. After several guesses well short of the true number, the speaker explained it in aviation terms. He said that a major airline would have to crash one fully loaded 747 jumbo jet every day for an entire year to match the annual deaths at that time from medical mistakes. That should give you some reference as to the safety record of commercial aircraft.

Medicine Takes Note

In the business of saving lives, many doctors and hospitals are now using the checklist approach and other practices of the airline industry to govern how they conduct medical procedures such as surgeries. Their goal is to reduce the number of medical mistakes or missteps and provide better quality medical care. Surgery preparation protocols are utilizing checklists, challenge and response verbal exchanges, and standardized operating procedures.

Dr. Sanjay Parike, a renowned pediatric surgeon in Seattle, WA, has been working on such a program for his medical teams. He showed me all of the protocols they go though as a medical team. Gone was the paradigm that the surgeon was the boss and everybody just listens to his orders. Instead, it was a team concept, and everyone got to have a voice in the procedure.

I got to witness this as he prepared my daughter for throat surgery recently. The team gathered in the prep room, and the surgeon called out the items on the checklist. Various technicians, nurses, and support doctors (anesthesiologist, etc.) answered in turn. We were asked several questions as well in order to cross-reference their data.

They checked and double-checked everything before our daughter ever went under. They even asked my daughter her name so they could verify it matched her hospital ID bracelet. They wanted to make sure they had the right patient!

Communication Can Save Your Life

Another doctor doing similar training work is my friend, Dr. Wendy Warwick, an anesthesiologist who works at a major hospital. She is teaching courses on methods for clearer communications and procedures so that any medical member can speak up. They use catchwords and phrases to get the attention of all involved and point out errors and issues during the medical procedure. The results have been astounding. According to Dr. Warwick:

> "The #1 cause of adverse effects in healthcare was problems in communication. This is where CRM comes into the struggle for safety in healthcare. Medicine has suffered for many years from the same hierarchal problems as aviation, and is beginning to benefit from some of the same team training strategies."

Man or Machine?

The medical field has many parallels to aviation in other ways as well. One of the more pronounced analogies that come to mind is automation versus the need for human interface.

We have some very incredible automated and medical surgical tools out there. But would you ever want a scan, X-ray, medical procedure, or surgery without a licensed professional monitoring you? Moreover, what if the machine made a mistake or wasn't working properly? What if the patient needed some reassurance?

One of the classic question I get as a pilot is "doesn't this plane pretty much fly itself?" Or the other classic is "You guys just turn on the autopilot and sit back, right?" For the record, there is hardly anything that the jets just do themselves.

A good comparison for the autopilot is the cruise control on your car. You still must have a plan of what your destination is, how you are going to get there, and the fuel that is required. You must prepare your car to drive by making sure the tires are inflated, there is adequate oil and fuel, the car's systems are working properly, etc. You need to monitor your speed, turn off cruise control when entering city streets, slow down for poor weather, reroute your plan for construction or road closures, and other such things.

It is the same with the airplane. The autopilot and other automatic functions on the airplane exist to relieve the pilots from task saturation and input overload. They don't replace the pilot, they help the pilot.

Imagine having to hold the control wheel for 5 hours straight. We'd be pretty fatigued doing that. By having the aid of some automated functions, we are able to focus on the more critical aspects of flight. It gives us more bandwidth in our minds to think about things like weather avoidance, fuel management, complicated airspace and approach procedures, Air Traffic Control (ATC) demands, and any aircraft problems that may arise.

So the best thing you can possibly say to your pilots (even better than "you look much younger and thinner since the last time I saw you!") is "Thanks for the safe flight!"

Planning to Fly

In order to best prepare for a flight, we pilots arrive into Operations at least one hour before departure. We print out all of the paperwork created by our dispatchers. These papers contain our current and forecast departure weather, forecast arrival weather, and the weather forecast at our alternate (diversion) airports. We know we will also get *en route* weather information such as winds, jet streams at altitude, and areas of significant weather.

The dispatch papers include a history of maintenance issues and repairs for the aircraft we are flying and any deferred items that are ok to fly with until they can be repaired at some later date. The dispatchers give us a report of NOTAMS (Notices to Airmen) that tell us of any runway closures or any significant items to be aware of for the airfields we are utilizing that day. We have a flight plan sheet that shows the number of the jet, the flight number, dispatch notes, aircraft performance factors, fuel burn for the route at different altitudes. On the sheet is a Fuel Summary section, which shows the fuel burn forecast to the destination, additional fuel for an alternate airport, holding fuel, taxi fuel, and the minimum required fuel (determined by the FAA).

Paperwork Drills

Once we review all of the paperwork, we must decide if we think changes need to be made before we fly. Examples of this would be requiring that a deferred item be fixed because we do not feel for this particular flight and circumstance that it is safe to fly with the item not repaired. Sometimes we may want to file a different route with ATC because we want a bigger margin of safety from areas of significant weather or turbulence.

Occasionally, we see issues with a NOTAM that we must plan around, such as runway closure or an approach navigational aid that is inoperative. We may also add additional fuel for such things as anticipated airport procedures, anticipated ground holds, early descents, and delays that we know may happen due to our experience with the departure or destination location. For example, a destination airfield that has only a single runway will prompt me to add fuel because there must be flexibility if that runway gets closed due to an on-field emergency preceding our arrival.

Once we've reviewed all plans, we sign a release saying that we agree to all of the final terms of the planning and to the fuel load (after our adjustments have been made).

Preflight

We then get to the jet about 45 minutes prior to departure and to do our preflight checks. That's typically when you passengers see us walk up to the gate. The flight attendants do a thorough cabin inspection, and the captain briefs the crew about the ensuing flight segment. We do a thorough cockpit inspection and an exterior walk of the airplane.

On the preflight walk, we inspect the fuselage, wings, nose, tail, skin surfaces, tires, brakes, wheel wells, hydraulic lines, engines, engine cowls, pitot tubes, static ports, antennas, lights, intake and exhaust valves, cargo doors, and just about everything we can visually see without taking the airplane apart. We then go to the flight deck and do a systems and warnings check to make sure the airplane can tell us if something goes wrong. We check to make sure all of the warning lights illuminate and all of the warning sounds work properly.

If anything is not working properly, we give maintenance a call. We then confer with the mechanics to decide if it's something that can be repaired or deferred for repair at another location.

Fixing and Troubleshooting

Repairs can take time. At some of the hubs, the airlines will keep some storage of spare parts. At stations away from the hubs, there are very few spare parts on hand, so the parts must be flown in if the mechanic cannot fix it.

Passengers have asked me many times when this happens, why we didn't realize there was a malfunction sooner. This is because we run the test about 30 minutes prior to departure, so it would be impossible to know any sooner unless the prior aircrew knew there was an issue and wrote up the problem in the maintenance forms.

Sometimes just troubleshooting the problem can take a while. Just as if your garbage disposal in your sink stops working, you must figure out the root cause in order to fix it. We too need to chase a problem down, but on an aircraft with hundreds of integrated systems, thousands of feet of fuel and hydraulic lines, and miles of wire, it takes time to figure it out.

From Preflight to Pushback

Once the preflight checks have been accomplished, we set up the jet for our specific flight. We position our seats, put out our navigational maps, set up our flight instruments, input our flight plan routing into the computer, and display all of the data we need for airplane performance and weight & balance.

We then recheck for the latest airfield conditions, acquire ATC clearance, get our fueling summary sheets from the ground crew, retrieve our final maintenance documents, and attain a release from our dispatch. The gate agent and flight attendant advise us of the final passenger count and any issues that may have arisen during the boarding process. We pilots brief each other about the flight and review imminent emergency procedures, such as having to reject the takeoff, engine failure or fire on takeoff, plus any special procedures unique to our current airfield, such as terrain avoidance or unique departure procedures.

We run our checklists, coordinate with the ground crew, and request pushback from the gate. We then push back from the gate and start the engines. After the engines are started, we begin our taxi to the runway.

Let's go Fly!

During the taxi on the airfield, while you are watching the safety demonstrations, we are running more checklists and doing final checks of the flight controls, hydraulics, engines, fuel, pressurization, and performance. Air traffic controllers watch our every move on the airfield and tell us what taxiway routing they expect us to take. Then we contact the tower controller for takeoff clearance. When the tower controller clears us onto the runway, we get into position and await takeoff clearance.

Once cleared, we push the throttles up and start down the runway. As we accelerate, we scan the instruments constantly and the environment outside to make sure the aircraft has good airspeed indications, the engines are performing correctly, and that we are accelerating properly.

During the takeoff roll, we are thinking of the airspeeds we are attaining and what they mean. There is a maximum speed that will allow us to abort a takeoff and still stop well before the end of the runway, there is another to lift off the ground, and yet another to climb out. Just know that as we roll down the runway, we are constantly thinking about the decision to continue the takeoff or abort in the case of an emergency, adjusting for winds, staying on the runway centerline, and making a smooth, controlled rotation from ground to flight.

Into the Sky

Once in the air we ensure we are climbing out at a specific airspeed and angle of attack. Then we retract the landing gear and check to ensure we are a safe distance from the ground and terrain. We then lower the nose, accelerate the aircraft, and bring the flaps up. Away we go!

The airport area is usually very busy, so we are constantly keeping situational awareness of other aircraft near us while ensuring that we are flying our proper route and ATC assignments. Once we are at cruise altitude, we are assessing winds, fuel, routing, weather, and turbulence. We then use our various navigational instruments (Global Positioning System (GPS), Inertial Navigation System (INS), and VHF Omni-directional Range (VOR) to fly along our highways in the sky. These highways are called Jet Routes over land and are called tracks over the oceans.

Once we are at altitude, we typically set the autopilot and pretty much let the airplane fly itself. That's a joke (we talked about this)!

Return to Earth

At the arrival area for the descent and approach, we are very engaged with the planning, preparations, and duties for successfully entering the airfield's airspace and negotiating their arrival procedures. We have step down fixes (a fix is a point in space), which we must cross at certain altitudes and speeds. They are somewhat like intersections in the sky.

Spacing is tight. There is just enough spacing between each jet for landings, clearing the runway, and any departures, so we have to stay on our toes. We brief our plan for descent including speeds, the active runway, turning off runway, and what to do if we have to go missed approach (go around).

A missed approach can happen for many reasons, so please don't be concerned if it happens. Sometimes it can be something as simple as the previous airplane being slow getting off of the runway. No big deal. We just circle back around and approach again.

We then run checklists, check the runway data, review the airport weather, and plan our taxi route to the airport gate.

The Right Stuff

As pilots, we need to have the ability to know where we are spatially, think ahead of the airplane, calculate distance and time quickly, and have good eye-hand coordination. These are especially critical skills to run simultaneously during the approach and landing phase. The autopilots and auto-throttles come off, our minds are thinking ahead, our eyes are scanning outside to the airport and then inside to our instruments. Our breathing is controlled, our arms are working the controls for the pitch and roll of the plane, and our feet are busy working the rudders for the yaw.

We work the airplane, adjusting for the wind gusts and any traffic in front of us. Then real art of the pilot happens - the approach, flare, landing and touchdown. At just the right moment we raise the nose and let the plane slowly settle down until it just kisses the runway (or at least that is what we try for!).

Smooth Operators

Now, some landings will be better than others. And sometimes it is better to make a firm landing than a soft one, like when the runway is wet or snowy. Sometimes you have a short runway and don't have the time or distance to work it like you would on a bigger runway.

Sometimes ATC wants you to land and turn off at a taxiway halfway down the runway, or they ask you to 'land and hold short (LAHSO)' of an intersecting runway. And sometimes we want to get on that early taxiway so we can cut 20 minutes off taxi time and get you to the gate quicker. Sometimes yes, it's just the pilot's skill and technique.

Just like friends that you drive with in cars - some are heavy on the brakes, jerky with the accelerator, or steer abruptly. Pilots can be that way too sometimes. Some are real smooth operators, and I like to think those techniques translate across into other skills and important areas of life!

What the Flight Attendants Tell You and Why

The flight attendants primary job is to keep us safe in the event of an emergency. When they are hired with the airline, they must demonstrate both safety and service skills. They are required to go through at least 6 - 8 weeks of initial training because they must be certified on all of airplane models that the airline utilizes.

On each model, they need to know the locations and use of emergency equipment and must be proficient in demonstrating how to respond to a variety of emergency situations. They attend annual refresher training courses in order to keep current. Their secondary job is to help us feel more comfortable with their service.

Each airline has a slightly different twist to their flight attendant duties, but the bottom line is that the flight crew, aircraft, and requirements must be in compliance with FAA regulations in order for the flight to operate.

Passengers and Luggage

Almost everything requested of you as a passenger has to do with some sort of safety mandate from either the FAA or the airline. When it comes down to luggage, we are all frustrated with what has transpired over the years. When we check in at the counter, none of us want to pay the extra bag fees. The FAA has a formula using an average number of pounds for each passenger, their checked luggage, and their carry-on luggage. This is the reason we are not required to step on a scale before each flight or weigh our luggage. Heavy bags make the aircraft burn more fuel, and fuel prices are generally high. So to help mitigate how much luggage weight people bring onboard, the airlines started charging the baggage fees.

From a safety perspective and for weight and balance planning for the airplane, we need to know if we are significantly over the FAA assumption of the average passenger weighing 175 lbs, the average checked bag weighing 50 lbs, and the average carry-on bag weighing 25 lbs. What happens now is that many people try to bring their entire luggage set as carry-on instead of checking some bags.

This is one reason that the boarding process takes much longer and overhead bin space quickly runs out. As a pilot, these weight assumptions are a concern, since it affects the performance of the aircraft as well as the fuel burn. I have seen a discrepancy as high as 10,000lbs on a 130 passenger aircraft that weighs 120,000lbs.

Boarding, Bags and Benevolence

When stowing our luggage, it is important to put only our luggage in the overhead bins perpendicular and not coats or hats, to allow the next person to have space for their carry-on bag. The flight attendants are no longer allowed to help us with this due to all of the injuries they have suffered from doing this in the past, both acute and chronic. They have been told by their parent airline that if they are injured in the process of helping to stow luggage, their workers compensation insurance will no longer cover them for their injuries.

If a flight attendant helps you in this manner, be sure to thank that person because they are doing it out of kindness and at their own risk. If you see a passenger struggling to stow a bag in the overhead bin and you are physically able, please consider lending a hand.

Safe In, Safe Out

The overhead bins must be completely closed and locked to prevent luggage from falling out at any time during aircraft operation. The area around your feet and your lap must be free and clear of objects between takeoff and landing. This is in case we need to emergency ground-evacuate the airplane.

The aircraft and the airline company are certified and must routinely demonstrate that people can egress the entire aircraft within 90 seconds. This short time period expectation is set by the FAA and is based on being able to escape fire and toxic smoke. When there is only one flight attendant per 50 passengers, it is very critical that there is nothing blocking our ability to undo our own seat belts, get out of our row, get to an escape exit, and go down the escape slide.

If we are seated in an exit row, we must know exactly what to do. The flight attendants ask us if we are able and willing to help in an emergency. If you nod your head and say yes, please understand you are now acting as an emergency coordinator in the event of an emergency.

The expectation is that you will quickly and effectively open the exit by removing the cover, pulling or rotating the handles, opening the hatch, evacuating yourself, and then assisting other passengers as they evacuate the airplane. You can be a hero and help save many lives, or not. That is why it is critical for you when seated in an exit row to actually read the emergency card in the pocket in front of you and really be prepared to act.

Realize that the most likely scenario for utilizing you would be a ground egress on the runway. In this scenario, the flight attendants will be too busy opening the main and aft entry doors and starting the evacuation to help you with your exit hatch or door.

Airwaves – Yours, Mine and Ours

Let's discuss cell phones and electronic devices. The FAA and the aircraft manufacturers say that no electronic devices are to be on for takeoff. There are several reasons for this. First, the aircraft is not allowed to push back from the gate until everything is off. This is in part due to the fact that everyone must be focused, watching and listening to the safety instructions being issued either by the flight attendants or on the video screens. Imagine if the worst were to happen and you don't even know where the closest exit is.

Secondly, when the aircraft are certified, they undergo a series of electromagnetic interference tests to make sure that the various radiating devices on the airplane (radar, radios, SATCOM, navigation, etc.) don't cause interference with the aircraft systems. Most all these transmissions come from antennas outside of the aircraft. So the manufacture designs the aircraft to shield what's inside the aircraft (avionics, flight computers, etc.) from what is radiating on the outside.

What is not tested are the several hundred people radiating cell phones, WiFi computers, and other devices from inside the airplane.

These emissions from the cabin can influence currents and voltages in wiring, magnetic instruments, and can interfere with radio transmissions and other aircraft equipment. Also, all onboard entertainment (audio, video, games, phones) is required to stop functioning (called an interrupt) when the flight crew makes a PA announcement (FAA requirement). Your personal audio and video devices do not do this, and so they don't comply with the FAA requirement, hence they stay off except when not in critical phases of flight. This is so the flight crew can relay life-saving information to you as needed.

Thirdly, if a signal is transmitted from an aircraft at altitude through a ground station, like a cell phone signal, this could block all of the cell users in a 200 Mile radius on the ground. The Federal Communications Commission (FCC) intervenes and the airline could face severe fines.

Believe me, the flight attendants do not want to have to badger us every flight to do what is required. So make sure to switch it off when they request it the first time. The good news is we have new technology that uses a cell node on the airplane that transmits all participating cell signals up to a satellite and then down to a ground station. So it may be possible to use cell phones onboard in the near future.

What You Want, When You Want It

Always know exactly where your life vest is. Who would have ever thought that an A320 domestic flight taking off out of New York would be in the Hudson River minutes after takeoff?

Also, be aware where your oxygen mask will fall. They will drop down if the cabin pressure altitude reaches 14,000 ft, as a safer breathing altitude is 10,000 ft or less. You have 12 minutes of oxygen, and this is plenty of time for the pilots to descend down below 10,000 ft if the aircraft is unpressurized.

If there is a rapid decompression, you will know it. The cabin will instantly get foggy and very cold. This is due to the pressure and temperature difference that existed with the outside air before the decompression.

Remember that you must put your mask on immediately. Your time of useful consciousness (TUC) is about 10-15 seconds at typical airline cruising altitudes. Once you are breathing through the mask, remember that the bag attached to the mask will not inflate, but oxygen is flowing to the mask.

In Case of Emergency

If we find ourselves having to rapidly evacuate the aircraft on the ground or at the gate, there are a few things to keep in mind. Always know exactly how many rows of seats there are to the nearest emergency exit. If there is a ground fire, the cabin can rapidly fill with smoke and you won't be able to see very well. In this case stay low and follow the emergency lighting on the aisle floor.

For an escape through a window exit over a wing, always do the 'leg, then body, then leg' maneuver, go to the back of the wing, and slide down the slide feet first. If you don't get out the window or door quickly, your fellow passenger behind you will probably expedite you, and it may not be pretty!

When exiting out through a slide, jump onto the slide feet first, straight legs, and arms folded across your chest. Yes, it will look steep from the top, but if you take any time to contemplate this or take your sweet time getting on the slide, you will likely get pushed by the person behind you. So keep moving!

All For One and One For All

If you are one of the first people out of the aircraft, stay at the bottom of the slide and help others at the bottom of the slide. Once away from the jet, form a group and stay together! The fire rescue crews are going to be looking for the exact passenger count to verify that everyone is off the aircraft. We don't want to put their lives at risk searching for a passenger that is already off of the aircraft. Realize that crewmembers are the last to exit the aircraft so it is your judgment and leadership we are counting on to help each other.

Pack and Dress for Safety

Storm Cattoche, an experienced flight attendant with a major airline, has many key points to share. She explains that it is critical to come prepared to the aircraft.

> "Make sure that you have any critical medications that you need with you at all times. Do not check them in with your luggage or even with your carry-on in case we must evacuate. Always have healthy snacks with you onboard, especially if you have any blood sugar issues or if you are traveling with children. Always wear clothing that is non-synthetic such as cotton or wool since nylons

and polyester can melt in high heat. If you want to be seen quickly in a rescue operation, white or red are the best colors to wear. You can also use pieces of those clothes as flags. I also always bring water with me and have two exit plans in case the first one is unusable."

Other clothing to mention is closed-toe shoes, which are much safer than flip-flops or spiked heels. As for common courtesy to your fellow passengers, it is not appropriate to be on the aircraft in sleepwear, micro-skirts, tank tops, halter tops, clothing with vulgar messages, or any other similarly offensive clothing. Since the airlines no longer provide blankets or pillows, wear comfortable layered clothing so you can best adapt as needed to the aircraft temperature. Make sure to coordinate ahead of time with the airline of any additional needs you may have such as a wheelchair, aisle chair, medical oxygen, etc.

Airline Operations

If there's one complaint I hear a lot from passengers, it's the "nickel and diming" they get when buying a ticket on a major US carrier. Again and again, the wallet is out to pay for a meal or snack, drinks, headsets, baggage fees, movies, etc. With the financial challenges after September 11, 2001, this became a necessary evil due to demand for the lowest ticket prices.

Let's take a look at air travel from the business perspective of the airlines for a moment. On the revenue side, ticket prices have not increased significantly relative to inflation since 1978. Meanwhile, costs at the airline have increased significantly. New aircraft, jet fuel, airport fees, facility costs, maintenance costs, and operating costs have gone up exponentially.

After September 11th, ticket prices plummeted. Airlines desperately scrambled to get passengers to simply fly again. Then SARS, the Iraq War, security fees, and higher fuel prices hit the aviation industry as well. Many airlines around the world just could not make it and went out of business. Many others found themselves in bankruptcy protection in order to restructure their debts and leverages. Many have been forced to merge in order to reap some economies of scale and stay alive.

All the while, ticket prices remained low, preventing these struggling entities from making any significant profits. Anytime an airline slightly raised the price, they would lose customers to another airline. One of the reasons this was happening was that the very practice of finding the lowest price was now in the hands of the individual consumer.

Pricing and Purchasing

Purchasing your airline ticket has undergone a series of major changes in the last 10-12 years. Gone for the most part is the visit to the travel agent to find you the best ticket for your travels. Online search engines, discount price bidding sites, and special 'online only' deals have made the Internet the new primary way to purchase air travel.

This enables folks to constantly and automatically scan the various ticket prices for the best deals. Back in the early 2000s, when the airlines were struggling, customers were able to somewhat control the pricing market by setting up alerts on their emails, cell phones, and instant messaging devices to notify them when a price point was reached. As the airlines bumped prices up, the consumer's automatic filtering would remove them from consideration.

Gone was brand loyalty, present was "get the best price with whatever route I have to fly or connections I have to make to get there."

Some of the low-cost carriers got crafty with how they listed their prices in order to get the most "hits" from these Internet search engines. They would list their prices without taxes, fees, and fuel surcharges. Unsuspecting consumers selected what they perceived as the lowest fare, but they were soon surprised when, for example, the special $99 fare turned out to be $139 after those costs were added back in.

Reducing Oversupply

Without the ability to raise prices, the airlines had to cut capacity. Cutting capacity has two benefits. Fewer seats available means that there will be more demand for those seats among consumers. With fewer alternatives, people will pay more to get one of those seats. Second, cutting capacity means fewer flights on a route per day, or using smaller jets to fly them versus the larger jets. This equates to lower operating costs.

Many of the airlines shrank excessively, giving flying to their code-share partners or handing routes over to smaller, contracted regional carriers. But shrinking capacity meant shrinking the airline itself, and about 50% of the airline labor force became unemployed. Some was done through massive furloughs (lay-offs), while other positions were eliminated through the use of contract labor.

The Shakeout and the Shakedown

In the pilot force, we watched as the government promised to help the ailing industry through guaranteed loans to the air carriers. Yet Congress only allocated around 5% of their promise. None of the large, major air carriers that applied for the loans were ever given aid. One by one, they fell. Some of us hoped for a temporary period of price regulation until the industry could recover, but that never came.

On top of these troubles, the airlines were forced to pay for the new TSA security requirements being mandated by the government following the terrorist attacks. For all these reasons, you are now paying for extra items that used to be included in the higher ticket prices.

Remember the good ol' days, when you would book a flight, arrive at the gate with minimal hassle, walk onboard to a smiling flight attendant? Do you recall being given exceptional cabin service, enjoying a hot inflight meal, and then stretching out in your empty row of seats in the 50 or 60% full aircraft? The airline was actually losing money on that flight.

Even with higher ticket prices, a 50% full aircraft is a loser in the revenue department. Depending on how the company is structured, the break-even point for load capacity is somewhere between 78% and 85%. With the reduction in capacity, airlines are now flying their airplanes mostly, if not completely, full. While that generates better profitability for the airlines, it can create havoc when a flight is cancelled and passengers need to be routed to other flights to complete their travel.

Putting Yourself in Good Hands

I have another question for you to ponder. Are you willing to pay a little bit more for your ticket to fly on a well-maintained jet, with a highly skilled and experienced flight crew? Please remember this when booking your trip.

When purchasing tickets on airliners, we should not use the same logic as buying a used lawnmower on Craigslist. This decision on who to fly with should be based more than just price alone. You are paying for a safe, positive experience when you travel by air.

Find the airline that has the best safety record, the customer service you require, the amenities you like, and the perks you enjoy (mileage, etc.). Understand which airline is actually operating your flight and what type of equipment they are operating. Sometimes that flight from New York to Dallas is a lot more comfortable on a new 737-800 than it is on an older DC-9 or a contracted regional jet.

The major U.S carriers typically have the most experienced pilots and flight attendants, and fly the newer, larger, well-maintained jets. Dave Warwick, a pilot for a major US carrier, advises that

> "Experience can literally save your life, saving a few dollars will not. Just because the jet is from a reputable company like Boeing or Airbus, does not mean you will get the most experienced and well-trained pilots at the controls. Your ticket selection on the carrier you trust is how you pick your pilots, flight attendants, and well-maintained jets."

Be aware if you are booking on a code share affiliate airline or a smaller regional carrier that is contracted by the major airline. You can tell this on the booking screen, if you see "Operated by XYZ Airlines" and the name is different than the major carrier. You may want to book a different departure time for your connection to stay on the major carrier's equipment, with its experienced crew, and quality.

Sometimes the flight number may not even change from one leg of a trip to another, but you will find yourself flying on a code-share or regional contract carrier. If this sounds confusing, call the major airline reservation hotline and they will be glad to assist you.

Positive Control of Luggage

When you arrive at the airport and check your luggage, a large sticky tag with a barcode is attached. The airlines now use laser scanners, similar to those used at checkout stands in the grocery store, both to track the location of the bag and to help the airline identify where the bag is destined to go. This has greatly reduced the amount of lost and misrouted luggage. Being able to track where the bag has been and where it currently is sitting allows for better airline customer service when a bag is lost. The airlines are also getting better with waiting for inbound connecting luggage to arrive in order to make sure it gets onboard the next leg of its journey.

With so many people now taking carry-on luggage into the main cabin in order to avoid baggage fees, the boarding and deplaning processes take longer than it has in the past. Unfortunately many of these passengers wind up gate-checking their bags due to limited overhead storage space. To date, the airlines are not charging to gate-check luggage.

On Time and On Your Side

Airlines vie for position in the marketing ranks of being the most on-time airline. The down side of this is when the focus shifts from good customer service to getting an on-time departure no matter what. Try looking at this for a moment from customer service representative's (CSR) point of view. A lot of airlines rate their job performance as how many flights they got off on time. So there is little motivation for them to stop what they are doing and give you 5 minutes, or even 2 minutes, of their time to answer questions.

Some airlines now have large digital displays at the gates showing the weather radar pictures, lists of upgrade requests and standby passengers, along with up-to-the-minute flight status. This has been a great aid for situational awareness and communication to the passengers in the waiting area. It relieves the customer service representative from having to answer these routine questions while they are trying to actively process and board awaiting passengers. This time savings results in better boarding performance and more on-time departures from the gate.

Many airlines have even instituted company policy to close the entry door to the airplane 10 minutes prior to departure time. Once the door is closed, the flight is closed (meaning you cannot add more passengers to the list or manifest) so no more late stragglers can board. This is why sometimes you can run for the gate and the plane is just sitting there with the jet way for several minutes, but they won't let you board.

The employees' performance is measured by the on-time departure from the gate, not accommodating passengers. Now, don't get me wrong, some agents will bend over backward to help you, but understand that there is little incentive to do so from their employer, so don't expect it. This is why it is very important for you to be in the gate area 45 minutes or more prior to departure time.

Be sure to board with your seat grouping so you are assured of getting your assigned seat. If they don't have a person physically in the seat, then they start giving the seats away to standby passengers 15-20 minutes prior to departure. So you really have to check the clock before you go make the run for that last-minute mocha latte.

Managing the Clock

The on-time departure clock usually starts when the pilots release the brakes, after coordinating with the aircraft tug crew. Many times if we are delayed out of the gate, there are several things that we can do as pilots to help make up some time. We can request a closer runway for takeoff (creating shorter taxi times). While in the air, we can ask ATC for 'cutting the corners' or taking shortcuts to shave off some time. We can keep the speed up if we have the extra fuel to burn or get different altitudes with more favorable winds if ATC agrees. We can fly a higher speed on descent and request a runway with the shortest taxi time to the arrival gate.

Sometimes the flight plans are already padded with some extra time cushion in case of delays. There are times, however, when we make all of these efforts in order to help you make tight connections and still we have to spend extra time unexpectedly deviating around weather, holding near the destination airfield, getting slowed down by ATC, or handling other logistics like not having a ground crew at the arrival gate to marshal us in. If you do miss your connection, you can immediately call the airline to have them rebook you on a later flight or speak in person to a customer service agent.

On-time arrival is considered to be anytime within 15 minutes of the scheduled arrival time. If you want to fly with less stress about making a connecting flight, try to schedule your flights with 2-3 hours between the arrival time of one leg of your trip and the departure time of the next one.

Remember, that doesn't mean you will be waiting the whole time. Sometimes the connecting gate is in a different terminal at the connecting airport. This allows you plenty of time to arrive late, find your new gate, and be ready to board with everyone else. If the first flight is on time, you will also have plenty of time to get some food and drink, visit the bookstore, and saunter over to your next flight.

Flight Frequency

There has always been a fine balance between what the customer wants and what the airlines can provide. When it comes to flight frequency, passengers would like the option to have a flight to their desired location every half an hour! But many barriers block the airlines' ability to provide this.

The airlines pay the airports and the cities for slots, as well as for landing fees. There are only a certain amount of slots in this air and ground real estate war, and the airlines compete against each other for these opportunities. The gate slots are similar to leases. Each company contracts for the rights to these slots at agreed-upon prices and times.

Let's use JFK airport in New York as an example. Say Brand X carrier has the rights to use 20 arrival slots at JFK. Brand X can choose if they want to use one of these slots for a large aircraft (like a 300-passenger 777) to/from London Heathrow or a smaller airplane (like a 110-passenger 737) to/from Grand Rapids, MI. The analysis is done to determine how many feeder flights and how many heavy international flights should use these coveted slots. Many times it makes more cost sense to use a larger jets to transport more people at one time, resulting in less frequent flights. Other times it makes more cost sense to fly smaller jets with less passengers but doing so with greater frequency.

Air Traffic

There is also an issue of Air Traffic Control (ATC) arrival and departure rates when it comes to aircraft spacing. Airports will only allow a certain number of arrivals per hour due to aircraft separation and spacing for safety. When the weather is good and we can see each other as we are on arrival to the runway, our minimum arrival spacing is 4 nautical miles (nm). This is just enough spacing for the jet in front to slow to its landing speed, touchdown, roll out, and turn off the runway to a taxiway before the next jet is ready to land.

If the weather situation reaches instrument conditions (low clouds, fog, etc.), the spacing must be increased since we cannot see each other and are operating on instruments. This slows the arrival rate allowed to the airport. Unfortunately, no one knows what the weather will be like several months out when the airlines build their schedules.

Most schedules are built with the good weather arrival rate assumption. So, if there is any actual weather in the vicinity of the arrival airfield, it slows everything down. This will have a ripple effect on the flight plans of downstream legs for that particular aircraft and those plans for connecting flights.

When it comes to weather and delays, the first priority becomes the aircraft that are in flight. When the weather causes the arrival rates to slow way down or if the airport gets closed down temporarily, the jets flying will go into holding patterns in the sky. Depending on the time needed to be in holding, the extra fuel onboard, and the sequence of where we are, we will either get cleared into the arrival airport or divert to another airport.

An Airport Is Not a Parking Lot

In the meantime, the aircraft that are on the ground and at the airport gates must stay there. Now, the airport can get overloaded with too many aircraft and not enough places to put them. This causes 'gate holds' or 'ground holds' or 'tarmac delays'.

There are a few situations that I want to discuss to help in your understanding. If we have just landed and there are no gates available, we will have to hold out on the taxiway until a gate does open. If we are in a situation where we are taxiing out from the gate to depart and the airspace or airport shuts down temporarily until the weather passes, we could be out on the taxiway in holding areas for a few hours until the weather clears along our departure route. Many times the reason we cannot return to the gate is because it is now occupied with an inbound aircraft.

In addition, if we do return to the gate, we lose our departure sequence. Let's say, for example, that we are number 5 in the line for takeoff when the airspace clears of weather. If we had returned to the gate, assuming it was even still available, we would lose our sequence in line for takeoff. This means that by the time we go back, let a few passengers off the airplane, and do a top-off refueling, we could now become number 25 in-sequence for takeoff. This would result in a substantial delay in the flight itself and cause countless passengers to miss their connections. It could also result in the flight being cancelled if the pilots or a crewmember exceed their allowed duty time.

There have been some very bad situations in the past with passengers being stuck on airplanes for very long periods of time. My own flights were not any of those because of my personal thoughts on the subject and special techniques I used when delayed. The new Passenger Bill of Rights now prevents airlines from keeping you on the aircraft for more than 3 hours.

Connecting

This is good from a passenger-empowerment standpoint. The downside is that the airlines don't want to pay the fees, so if they anticipate extended holds, they are more likely to cancel the flight and deplane the passengers. So you might get a hotel for the night, but you end up departing probably a day later instead of a few hours.

A constant concern passengers have during operations like this is the connecting flights. Please remember that if the whole airport is being affected, then your connecting flight is being affected as well. That aircraft is also arriving inbound from somewhere else most likely, so it too will probably be delayed coming in to its gate. You still have a good chance of making it, so keep trying.

The flight attendants or pilots know very little in regard to these connections, other than perhaps what gate they are departing from. Occasionally, we can request info for a specific flight, but we are usually too busy trying to safely operate the aircraft. Remember that safety always comes first!

Safety and Security

In the aviation industry, safety is the first and foremost priority. Safety is the culture and the foundation upon which we build. In many other industries, safety is important. In ours, it is critical.

One of the key words we use when we refer to safety is redundancy. As I previously discussed in both the **Jets** and **Pilots** chapters, having backup functions are critical in operating aircraft. The aircraft themselves have the redundancy of backup systems, and the pilots back up each other. The reality is that you would die ten times in a car accident just driving to the airport before you ever got a scratch from an aircraft incident.

It is our job as pilots to decide whether or not we feel it is safe to fly in a given set of circumstances. We have the final and ultimate say when it comes to the Go or No-Go decision.

Backups, Deferrals and Decisions

In many cases, where a flight is delayed or cancelled due to a mechanical situation, it may not be that the aircraft cannot be flown safely in its current state. It may be instead that the backup system is not working. The airline, the mechanics, even the FAA guidelines may say that the item can be deferred. This means that we are allowed to fly now and fix it later when a specific date or scheduled maintenance period is reached. But ultimately, the people who are allowing deferrals get to drive home that night to their families, while we pilots have to determine what the real risk is based on many factors. If we feel the risk is too great, then we can refuse the airplane until a certain item is fixed.

There is a lot of pressure put on us by the airlines to fly aircraft with deferrable items because delaying or cancelling flights obviously costs a lot of money. There is also a lot of pressure put on us by the passengers who want to get to their destinations. Please remember that we too have families, friends, and important life events that we want to attend. Even so, when we don't feel comfortable with the situation, we will always lean to the conservative side of safety.

The aviation safety record to date has been nothing short of outstanding. We need to remember not to take this for granted! It is easy to forget, in our rush to get to our destinations, that we are flying in an airplane, and we need to be smart. So please, do not take your frustrations out on the ticket agents or the flight attendants. They are only trying to do their jobs to help you as much as they can. We will do our best as pilots to keep you advised as to what is going on. If you feel that this is not happening, and provided that we are still on the ground, ask the flight attendants or agents if the pilots, work permitting, can please give updates every 20 minutes or so.

Safety First

As mentioned in the Pilot chapter, we arrive one hour or more prior to departure. We review the preflight papers in order to catch any issues ahead of time. A comprehensive check of the airplane is accomplished and maintenance logbooks are reviewed.

Sometimes we are notified ahead of time that a maintenance issue is being worked on, but most of the time we do not know of any problems until we have performed our preflight duties. At this time, we contact maintenance and confer with them about the decision to defer, fix, or replace any item that is an issue. Occasionally, if we cannot do any of these, we must choose whether to wait until a part can be flown in, cancel the flight, or possibly move to another airplane. If the flight is cancelled, the airline will book you on another flight. We would much prefer to handle a maintenance issue on the ground than to have an in-flight emergency and divert to another airport.

When It Matters Most

Very rarely, we do have a situation *en route* that can be very serious. This is where our experience, knowledge, training, and skill come into play. Our foundation training is to "aviate, navigate, and communicate." This means that first and foremost, we fly the airplane, making sure we have pitch, power, and control of the jet. We do whatever we need to do in order to ensure this is happening.

After focusing on the aviation, we navigate and communicate. Navigating means we make sure the direction and path we are going is the most prudent way under the circumstances. Then we communicate with Air Traffic Control, dispatch, maintenance, flight attendants, and you passengers in order to let you know the situation. We also do this to coordinate a plan of action using all of our resources.

If we must divert to a different location, whether it is because of a maintenance issue, medical emergency, passenger security, weather, or fuel, we take into account several airports near our location. These airfields must support the size of jet we are flying, have adequate weather for approach and landing, and not have any significant notices to airmen (NOTAMS) about runway closures or navigational aids out of service.

Sometimes, the alternate airfields may not have the ideal passenger supports, but they are the safest choice under the circumstances. In these events, we may have to wait a while to bring the issue to completion and get everyone on their way. I hope we always ask for your patience and understanding.

Heroes and Zeros

I recall a time when we took off from a major airport and our secondary flight controls jammed. After advising ATC, we circled nearby while we tried many things to remedy the situation. We used our checklists, conferred with maintenance, communicated with all parties, but to no avail. We declared an emergency and returned to the airport from which we had originally departed.

Knowing that we were going to land at a significantly higher speed and somewhat overweight, we needed a much longer runway length than usual for landing. Our adrenaline was pumping as we brought the fully loaded airplane down, safely and smoothly. I could hear everyone clapping and cheering in the cabin. Yes, it was a job well done, and I give all those folks our thanks for their cooperation and calm.

Once we reached the gate and completed our shutdown checklists, we were told by the ticket agent who came onboard that we had been the last takeoff of the night. There were no other aircraft for anyone to take to continue their trip. The airline was going to cancel our flight and rebook all of the passengers for a flight in the morning. They also informed us that there were no hotel rooms for the passengers, due to several large technical conventions taking place in the area.

When the agent made that announcement, the passenger cheers turned to boos as we instantly went from heroes to zeros. It was frustrating and saddening for everyone. The solace for me was that at least everyone was safe because we did our jobs that day.

See Something? Say Something!

There are many ways in which you can help in the safety process. This is especially true if you are a frequent flyer, familiar with the way things should look, sound, and feel. If you experience anything at all out of the ordinary, please do not hesitate to say something to a flight crewmember about your concern.

A passenger once spoke up about a glove and a wrench sitting on top of an engine cowl before a flight. That large wrench could have destroyed the blades of the engine had it fallen into the engine intake during taxi or takeoff. Another time that I can recall, a passenger mentioned shortly after landing that he heard a grinding sound as we descended and that the back part of the wing was transitioning in a jerky motion instead of moving smoothly. When I insisted that maintenance take a look, they found that the trailing edge flaps were binding on that side and were about to seize. Aside from that passenger's report, there was no way we could have known this until the next flight, when the flaps would have failed.

Is There a Doctor On Board?

Another way you can help is in a medical emergency. We want everyone to be as healthy as possible by taking the best care of ourselves that we can. I tried to capture some of these tips and guidelines in the Travel Health chapter of this book. Airline travel can be stressful and taxing on our bodies, with the various temperature changes, dry and thin cabin air supply, exposures to bacteria and viruses. Plus the pure logistics of traveling itself can run us down. We need to stay ultra-hydrated and adequately nourished when we fly.

It is also important to ensure your immune system is strong when you travel so you won't be susceptible to disease. Always bring critical medications with you onboard the airplane. If you know that you have breathing issues, you can arrange ahead of time to have medical oxygen onboard the aircraft.

The Good Samaritan laws have thankfully protected people who work in the medical community. The flight attendants are not typically trained or skilled in first aid or CPR, so we rely on you medical personnel onboard to step forward with offers of help in the case of a medical emergency. We now have automatic defibrillators aboard the aircraft and in some airports nationwide. There are also basic first aid kits as well as a medical kit onboard.

If needed, we can set up a conference call with a doctor on the ground to help determine the severity of the situation. They can help us decide if we need to divert in order to get a passenger to the hospital quickly. In these situations, we ask all passengers to think of your loved ones - how you would want us to do everything possible to help them and get immediate attention if they were the ones who needed it. This is far more important than the inconvenience of delays to our travel plans. You'll help us by staying calm and helping each other when the aircraft needs to divert for a medical emergency or death onboard.

Security Briefing

Let's discuss security. There are many items I would like to address, but I cannot. A lot of our security procedures are very sensitive information, designed to protect all of us. Several pilots who have spoken up about this subject have been reprimanded and grounded for trying to point out holes and lapses in the security protocols. The bottom line is that pilots rely on these security measures to protect our airports, jets, passengers, and crew.

Many things have changed since the horrific events on Sept 11, 2001. We must all go through extensive security screening now. The liquid, shoe, and body scanner procedures became necessary, unfortunately, due to repeated attempts to wage attacks against our safe skies. If you are concerned about any radiation from the scanners, you can elect to have a pat-down instead. Just plan some extra time for this.

Chuck Thomas, a pilot for a major airline and instructor in crew self-defense, says:

> "There are numerous layers of protection that comprise civil aviation security. Airport security screening checkpoints are only one component of this multi-layered system of protection visible to the traveling public. At the national level, there are a number of organizations and resources that work constantly to develop and analyze intelligence, coordinate information and responses to potential threats, and share reciprocally the data with counterpart organizations in various countries. At the Federal level, there are several operational units that include the Federal Air Marshal

Service (FAMS) and the Federal Flight Deck Officer Program (FFDO). The Air Marshalls are specially trained to ensure the safety and security of the US aviation system. The FFDOs are airline pilots who receive special federal law enforcement training, are qualified to carry firearms, and are certified to use those firearms and defensive tactics to defend against any criminal or terrorist attempt to take control of an aircraft. These pilots volunteer their time and money for this training and are not paid for their participation in this program. Each airport also has comprehensive security plans and protocols. The asset that is the most vital to aviation security is the traveling public. Passengers can be the eyes and ears by being observant and alerting authorities to suspicious individuals or activities. If the crew requires extra assistance during a situation, passengers can be a valuable resource in helping to protect the flight".

The TSA has done a very good job of intercepting and thwarting terrorist attempts on our aircraft. I personally feel there is much more to do if we are completely serious about full protection, but these initiatives take both manpower and money. So we walk this fine line between what is overreaching our privacy rights and what is necessary for safety.

Cockpit Safety

Some aircraft have been equipped with barricades to help block cockpit access when we must open the flight deck door for a few seconds. However, some airlines are uninstalling them to save money! In any case, we cannot have any passengers in the forward galley areas of the flight deck, except for quick ingress or egress of the lavatory.

The best security we have is you, the passenger. If you see, smell, hear, or sense anything that is concerning to you please immediately speak up. Tell the gate agents if you experience anything in the boarding area. Tell the flight attendants if you are witness to something in the jetway or on the airplane during the boarding process. Insist through customer feedback that your airline install safety measures onboard the aircraft such as cockpit barrier devices.

Spring-Loaded

We are primed as a flight crew, spring-loaded you might say, to immediately remove anyone from the aircraft who we deem to be a threat, whether through actions, words, or behaviors. Much as we care about you, the airplane is not really the place for humor and gentle social management – that's for gate agents. I can think of a story when a passenger was standing at the gate counter yelling at the gate agent out of frustration. The passenger yelled loudly "Do you know who I am?" The gate agent proceeded to pick up the microphone for the passenger address system and announced to everyone in the boarding area "Does anybody know this man? Because he does not seem to know who he is." Everyone laughed, the man turned beet red, and I am positive he never said that again!

When the flight attendants greet you at the entry door to help coordinate seating and carry-on luggage, it is not just to be friendly and helpful. This is also to assess any odd, unusual, or erratic behavior. People have been removed at the gate for having too much alcohol or taking too many medications. This is because the crew simply does not know if that person will turn belligerent, violent, or incapacitated. We will not put the safety of all the passengers and crew at risk, on the ground or in the air.

Any sort of verbal or physical assault by a person against any agent, crewmember, or fellow passenger will not be tolerated. This will result in removal from the flight and possible arrest with federal charges filed.

When reporting unusual events, you can use words such as 'concerning' or 'suspicious.' Those should be investigated immediately, so demand that they are. It is much easier and safer to handle a situation on the ground than in flight.

We expect that you, too, will be spring-loaded to help if we are *en route* and a situation arises that threatens the safety and security of the flight, the crew, or the passengers. It is much more effective to quickly suppress and immobilize a violent or dangerous passenger with 5 people than it is for one person to attempt it. Remember, no one can open exterior doors or windows in flight due to the pressure difference, and a small hole will not cause a rapid decompression. We are all on the same security team, and this is our flight!

The Weather

The most common discussion that comes up with passengers, family, and friends is turbulence. Let's discuss first what it is exactly. As changes in air temperature take place, so do the densities of the air. This creates air currents and pockets, just as it does in an ocean.

There are different types of turbulence. Mechanical turbulence comes from air currents disrupted by structures such as mountains, buildings, and obstructions. Convective turbulence is born from the rise of hot air due to the heating of the ground. These lifts or columns are called thermals.

Cold air is more dense so it tends to sink; warm air is conversely less dense and tends to rise. This is why, in a two-story home, the downstairs floors are typically much cooler than the upper floors. This is essentially how cold fronts and warm fronts operate.

A great example is the cool, dense air that flows down from Canada that eventually meets the warm, moist air flowing up from the Gulf of Mexico. Where they tend to meet is in the central plain states of the United States. And that is exactly where you find some of the most active weather systems and turbulence in the country.

Big Clouds

As the cold air meets warm air, it slides underneath it, pushing the warm air upward. This makes the entire ground-to-space column of air unstable and builds large towering clouds that sometime develop into thunderstorms. Occasionally, these storms will have rotating effects that can cause roll clouds or tornadoes.

We do our constant best to avoid any building cumulus clouds, just as we try not to fly across weather fronts. In our preflight planning, we look at all of the weather charts, current conditions, forecasts, and radar pictures to analyze the best altitude and route to take in order to avoid these weather situations. Once we are flying, we also request and receive pilot reports through our dispatch, ATC, even directly from other airplanes up ahead on the route in front of us.

We can usually see buildups of clouds and can visually avoid them during the day. At night, we rely on our weather radar to show us areas of convective activity and precipitation to avoid. Remember that no matter how bumpy the turbulence, the airplane will never just fall out of the sky or break apart in flight. We pilots will do our best to minimize the impacts of the weather that our flight will have to deal with. Just know that it's part of the flying experience, so we are trained extensively for it.

The Jet Stream

Other ways we can tell about different air currents and the potential for turbulence is through abrupt changes in air pressures, temperatures, and wind direction or speed. The weather reporting systems are so advanced now, including the onboard systems, that it helps us to better anticipate bumpy air than we've been previously able to do. These changes in air characteristics help us to know where the jet stream is as well.

The jet stream is sort of like a large river in the sky. Typically air flows on a large scale across the US from west to east. This is why it will take you only 5.5 hrs to fly from San Francisco to New York, but 6 hrs for the return trip back to the west. When flying with the current of the jet stream, we try to take advantage of the tailwind.

The disadvantage of getting close to the jet stream, however, is that the boundaries around it can be quite turbulent. Flying in this area may cause us to encounter clear air turbulence (CAT). Every once in a while, we will experience this because we can only predict and forecast so well.

Waves and Chop

Flying through turbulence can be disconcerting because it is sometimes unexpected and may seem like speed bumps in the sky. Try to think of the air as you would the surface of a lake or ocean. There are currents that flow. The stronger the currents, the more temperature and density differences you have. The water gets choppy. Wind, which is actually a lower density fluid than water, also creates waves and chop in the surrounding air, just as it does on the surface of the water.

Like taking a boat on the lake, your airplane goes through waves and chop in the air. If the water you're sailing is wavy or choppy, you don't notice it much if you are on a cruise ship, but you sure feel it if you are riding in a rowboat. In aviation, the larger the airplane, the more stable it is, so it's less likely you will feel as much of the effects of the unstable air in a jetliner. Fly in a small airplane, and you'll definitely feel more of the bumps.

Turbulence and other weather phenomena can never be predicted with 100% accuracy. In general, however, the seasons of spring and fall tend to have less convective activity and snow/ice effects.

Location, Location, Location

Certain routes tend to be more turbulent than others because of their departure and arrival locations. Places such as Reno, Boise, Denver, Maui, Juneau, and Palm Springs have their own ecosystems, with terrain and wind flows that tend to make it somewhat more turbulent to fly in and out. People who do not travel frequently to these locations are not familiar with the dynamic weather and may get frightened when flying through it. Brace to manage the discomfort, but talk yourself out of the fear. As uncomfortable as it can be, we fly through these conditions all the time and would never put the aircraft in an environment that is unsafe.

Thunderstorms

We avoid thunderstorm activity and its effects as much as we possibly can. Inside of these weather cells are some of the most severely turbulent conditions, due to vertical changes in airflow. The classifications of the severity of these cells range from 1 to 6. Level 5 and 6 storms generate very heavy rains, hail, thunder, lightning, tornadoes, and extreme wind shear.

Occasionally, these storms move faster than forecast, or new cells will pop up along our route. We can coordinate with our company dispatchers and ATC to deviate off our course in order to avoid flying in or near these storms. Sometimes, they grow so fast that they merge together in a row. In weather terms, this is called a squall line.

If we know our route is transitioning a squall line, we typically add extra fuel so we can deviate as required to find the best airspace through the line of storms. If the squall line extends across many states, it may be difficult to find a way through. As we approach it, we are studying and analyzing it with our onboard weather radar to find the safest area to fly across. Sometimes we may fly parallel to the line in order to find the safest area through it.

Penetrating this kind of weather takes patience. As we find corridors to fly through, we then fly through the path of least resistance - in pilot terms, we 'shoot the gap.' This is where you may feel some of the effects from the adjacent weather pattern. We try to keep these transitions to the shortest duration we can.

We stay at least 20 miles upwind of the thunderstorm cells. Plus, we stand off from the anvil-shaped top of a storm cloud an extra mile for every 10 knots of wind speed.

Much Better Safe Than Sorry

We never take off if thunderstorms are on or very near an airport. We also never fly an approach to landing if there are thunderstorms on our path. This is because of the turbulence and wind shear associated with these cells. These can affect the performance of the aircraft and can create a flying condition from which recovery may be difficult, if not impossible. That's hard for a pilot to admit. To avoid unmanageable flight situations due to weather, we will delay our takeoff at the airport gate, the taxiway, or the runway until the cells and their effects move away from the airfield.

When facing these conditions in the air, we are likely to be given a holding pattern from ATC, asking us to wait from a distance for the weather to pass in order to assure a safe approach and landing. Occasionally, it may be necessary to deviate to another airport, refuel, and then return to flight once the weather is clear at the destination airfield. I know it can be frustrating and inconvenient when weather delays or cancels a flight, but respecting the weather is the only intelligent course. Our safety depends on it.

Special Effects

Sometimes when we fly in areas of convective activity, static electricity builds up. Just like when you rub a balloon in your hair or slide your socked feet over new carpet, friction creates a charge that eventually dissipates electrically. The air rubbing against the aircraft skin creates the same phenomena. An electric charge builds up on the aircraft. The jets have many devices, such as static wicks on the aft edges of the wings and tail, to dispel this electricity.

Once in a while, the charge builds faster than it can be dissipated; then we get a phenomenon known as St Elmo's Fire on the cockpit windshields. It is amazing to see, since it looks like blue lightning dancing along the windows. If it builds too fast, a white flash or ball can suddenly pass through the aircraft as an electrical discharge. This will not harm the jet, its equipment, or the passengers.

Lightning

Lightning strikes always make passengers uneasy, and rightfully so. Lightning can be extremely hazardous to both people and equipment. However, there are some things you should keep in mind as the uneasiness passes.

Commercial airliners are designed to handle lightning strikes. They have internal paths within the skin and structure to safely move lightning from wherever it strikes to a safe location for dissipation. This current path is designed to keep the lightning effects away from people and equipment, allowing it to transition safely out of the airplane.

Composite airliners have embedded network of metal cables and wires to do the same. In fact, the airplane manufacturers have large lightning labs where they test the susceptibility of the airplane's structures and systems. Usually there is no action required by the pilots if an aircraft is struck by lightning, other than to report it to maintenance. After the flight, it could be necessary for the mechanic to do an inspection to make sure there was no charring of the skin or small holes at the points of lightning entry and exit.

Hail

Hail can be unnerving - very loud and distracting when flying through it. Just like the damage it can do to your car, hail can dent the aircraft skin, wrinkling its smooth contours. This has a small impact on the aircraft's aerodynamic performance. Dimples in the aircraft skin can cause more drag when the aircraft is flying, so more fuel is burned. Not to worry, these effects are usually minor, and the aircraft will fly just fine.

Large thunderstorms can throw hail for many miles. We typically try to avoid areas of forecast hail, but sometimes clouds surprise us and we find ourselves flying through hailstones. If the hailstorm occurs while we are on the ground, typically a mechanic will inspect for any damage before the decision is made to take the airplane or ground the aircraft until it can be repaired.

How Are We Supposed to Drive In This?

Heavy rain, snow, and ice will affect the performance of the aircraft. When you are driving your car on the freeway in these conditions, you drive much slower to avoid hydroplaning or to counteract increased braking distance. Similarly, in moderate or heavy rain conditions, we will not take off or land an aircraft because of degradation of braking and controllability on the runway. Also, the engines have reduced performance in heavy rains due to the increased water weight on the airplane, influx of hydro components to the engines, and the friction of moving through standing water.

In the winter months, snow and ice create slushy or slick runways that can degrade takeoff and landing performance as well as performance of the aircraft itself. Airports always attempt to de-clutter runways and taxiways of snow and ice, but sometimes it is so heavy that the removal equipment just cannot keep up.

Winter Requires De-Icing

To handle the wintertime conditions, we will de-ice the aircraft either at the gate or at a de-icing area location on the airfield. Ice affects the weight, shape, and surface of the aircraft, so it must be removed before takeoff. We use different types of fluid that are sprayed onto the jets. Some of the treatments are de-ice formulas to remove existing ice, while some are anti-ice formulas to help prevent ice buildup.

Once we have been de-iced and are taxiing to the runway, we will stop to have one of the pilots go back in the cabin to do a wing check. I call it the lap dance because we often have to slide into some of the passenger rows to get a good look at the wing surfaces. Being smaller, I have to slide way into the row to see what I need to see.

We check the top, forward, and aft surfaces of the wings as well as the flight control surfaces to make sure they are visibly clear of ice prior to attempting a takeoff. They are adequately de-iced when they look shiny and smooth all over, not dull or opaque. I should mention that some of the airlines are doing away with this protocol.

I recall being at the airport gate one winter day. A passenger came up to the cockpit after we had been de-iced at the gate and said, "Excuse me, I don't want to interrupt but I don't think those men spraying the jet out there sprayed off your left wing, and it looks like they've already left." I immediately went back into the passenger cabin and sure enough, he was correct. They had managed to miss the entire left side of the jet. We were very grateful that he spoke up right away when he saw something unusual.

No Ice, Thank You

When flying, we try to avoid any areas of moderate to severe icing, and we reduce the amount of time we spend in known icing conditions. These ice conditions typically occur at a very small range of altitudes that sit right at the freezing temperatures of water. Any ambient temperature less than 10 Celsius, with visible moisture present, indicates the need to turn on our engine de-icing systems.

We watch for visible buildup of ice on the nose section of the aircraft to let us know when to turn on the wing de-icing systems. Hot air is bled off of the engines in order to heat the aircraft surfaces and keep ice off. We can also sometimes change to higher and colder altitudes to fly out of the areas of moisture, or we can descend to a lower, warmer altitude. We may delay putting flaps and gear out on the approach to reduce the amount of time these surfaces are exposed to icing conditions.

Low Visibility

Low visibility such as heavy fog or white-out conditions can delay a flight or arrival. The technology for dealing with this is amazing in the precision of the navigational aids and equipment on the aircraft. We have the ability to do low-visibility takeoffs as long as we can see ahead of us in order to effectively steer down the runway.

In these situations, we plan for a takeoff alternate airport in case something goes wrong such as an engine failure on takeoff. In the event that occurred, we could not return to the takeoff airport for landing because of the low visibility. Instead, we could fly on one engine to another airfield nearby with better weather conditions and land there.

In order to land in marginally low visibility circumstances, we must have all of our main systems and navigation systems operating normally. Modern jets flown by the major airlines have the capability to "auto land." We program the autopilots and flight guidance systems to fly an Instrument Landing System approach. The ILS provides very precise electronic guidance both vertically and laterally to a touchdown point on the runway.

The pilots continuously monitor all aircraft and navigation system parameters all the way to landing and rollout. We are always prepared to intervene in case of any malfunction. We must be able to perform a missed approach at any moment, which means we take over from the auto land systems and get the plane climbing immediately should there be any hiccups on the approach.

The airlines pay a lot of money to possess and maintain these automated landing systems so that aircraft can land safely in a greater variety of weather conditions. The autopilot and auto-throttle systems that comprise the auto land systems must be working with fine precision (both the primary and backup systems). Without these systems working, airlines would not be able to land at destination airports in low visibility or low cloud ceiling conditions.

Weather Affects Everyone

It is a very good idea to keep an eye on the Weather Channel the day before your flights to see what the weather is doing. If it looks like there may be some significant weather, call the airline the day of your flight before heading out to the airport. Check on the status of your flight to ensure it is not delayed or cancelled. This may prevent you from having to wait for hours at the airport.

Sometimes flights are delayed even in good weather because the jet you are waiting for may be delayed in its previous location due to weather conditions, air traffic control issues, or maintenance. Always pad your flight plans with 3 or more hours for your arrival, or even a day if you can. I have seen too many people melt down because of not meeting planned arrival times for things like cruise ship departures, wedding appearances, baby arrivals, important meetings, funerals, graduations, and other once-in-a-lifetime events. The airlines, the aircrew, and the gate agents have no control over weather or ATC, but you can rely on us to make sure you fly safely.

Life is too short to endure unnecessary stress, so give yourselves plenty of cushion or an alternate plan if you possibly can!

Travel Health

At the airport and inside the jets, we are exposed to many health situations that are somewhat different to our everyday life. Our immune systems are challenged continually by dehydration, stress, fatigue, bacteria, and viruses. The best thing that we can do during air travel is to support our immune responses so that we can keep functioning at our best.

Staying Hydrated

Dehydration is one of the most important factors for optimum health. It is also one of the most often overlooked. Most aircraft have cabin air humidity levels of only 4% when inflight. So even if you were hydrated when you stepped onto the aircraft, you become dehydrated very quickly after only a short period inflight.

A large majority of passengers make the problem worse by drinking coffee, alcohol, and sodas which can act as diuretics to dehydrate you even further. Usually, by the time you feel thirsty, you are already far too dehydrated. We often hear the recommendation that we should drink eight 8oz glasses of water per day. When you travel by air, you should drink even more.

The absolute best type of water you can drink is the ultra-filtered, extremely hydrating, alkaline water. The pH and purity is significantly greater than bottled water or the water from your faucet. This ionized water is broken down into micro-clustered molecules so that our bodies immediately begin absorbing it.

This water also helps to neutralize acids in our bodies, thus reducing inflammation and encouraging new cell growth. Many health issues and symptoms we deal with - such as fatigue, acid reflux, asthma, intestinal and colon problems, blood sugar factors, joint pain, muscle aches, insomnia, and bloating - result from the body's creating an inflammatory response. When researching on the Internet, we find that an inquiry with the words "can cancer grow in an alkaline body?" will result in multiple links to articles from researchers explaining the science of why it cannot.

Hundreds of thousands of people have changed the course of their health globally by having a more alkaline, less acidic diet, including the use of high pH ionized water. If you want more information, go to Leinsetler@skyhydrate.com.

Anti-Inflammatory Eating

As for foods while traveling, anything that will create bloating - high sodium, preservatives, sugars, or acidic foods - are going to make you feel fatigued because of the inflammation it creates. Choose light, healthy foods such as fresh, colorful veggies, lean meats, nuts, seeds and whole grains. It may be difficult to find around some airports, but you must stay committed to eating healthier so that you can feel better, more alert and energetic. Companies like The Plant Café serve great tasting, organic, healthy foods. You can find one in Terminal 2 at the San Francisco International Airport.

As we start to take back control of our health, longevity, and functioning, the market will drive more of these types of food providers into existence. Stores such as Phountain Health promote the alkaline lifestyle. I personally love these stores because they provide alkaline water for super hydration and acidity reduction, greens to boost your antioxidant levels, colloidal micro- and macro-nutrients for cell growth and support, supplements, as well as services such as infrared saunas, massage, ionic footbaths, etc. for detoxification. Check out www.PhountainHealth.com.

Solar Radiation

Radiation is a concern for many flight crews and passengers, since we are routinely exposed to solar radiation at the high altitudes at which we fly. A corporate jet captain friend of mine did some research on this pilot exposure issue. He found that on a day of low solar activity (few solar flares, etc.), a flight at 41,000 ft across the United States subjects a pilot to nearly the same levels of radiation as a dental X-ray. The figures for this calculation come from a National Aeronautics and Space Administration (NASA) website that relates planned flight date and altitude to anticipated radiation levels. Since we cannot wear lead suits, we must find ways to boost our body's tolerance of radiation through antioxidants, alkalinity, hydration, oxygenation, circulation, and detoxification.

Air at Altitude

Pressurization makes for another interesting subject. Most aircraft collect air through intakes on the bottom of the aircraft. This air is then compressed and pumped into the cabin so that the equivalent altitude in the cabin stays relatively low compared to the outside air, generally not greater than 8,000 ft MSL. If it weren't for this pressurized air, the cabin air would be thin, like on a very high mountain, and there would not be enough pressure to push air into your lungs. Passengers would have to be on supplemental oxygen masks the whole flight, making eating and drinking a real challenge! Plus there are physiological effects at high altitudes – namely, hypoxia and altitude sickness.

Even with pressurization, the cabin pressure altitude is fairly high, like a ski resort in the Rockies, so there are some effects that you can feel. This pressure altitude can affect some people more than others, creating a feeling of light-headedness. This is also why you become a little sleepy and maybe even a little groggy on the flights.

If the cabin pressure altitude starts going higher than this setting, the pilots get a warning and we will immediately start a descent to a lower altitude to increase air pressure. Overhead oxygen masks will drop if the cabin pressure altitude goes above 14,000 ft. In that situation, passengers will be able to breathe oxygen until a safe altitude is reached.

Protecting Your Ears

Most people can handle the cabin air pressure changes on the ascent. However, the descent can be tough on people who have little, sensitive ears, like me. This is why a perfectly behaved baby or toddler on a flight may start to cry as we descend and approach the destination airport. Chewing, sucking, drinking, swallowing, and yawning can help relieve the pressure building inside of your ears and equalize it with the cabin pressure.

As the cabin pressure altitude is constantly changing during descent, travelers must continue equalizing to stay ahead of the air pressure. Other techniques that work are moving your lower jaw forward or doing the Valsalva maneuver (pinch your nose closed, close your mouth, push air pressure to your ears by blowing into your cheeks and ear canals).

You can also try my monkey ear technique. Grab firmly the cartilage of your ears right where they join to your head. Pull each ear strongly outward, then move it in circles as large as possible. Do this several times. You are literally stretching your ear canal, so it may feel uncomfortable as you pull and yank your ear. If you are doing it correctly, you will feel the relief inside your ear as the pressure differential equalizes.

Grounded By a Head Cold

You should never fly with a head cold, since the cold will inflame your sinus and ear cavities and prevent you from clearing your ears. I once flew as a very sick passenger when in my teenage years. I didn't know that I had double pneumonia and that my right ear canal was swollen shut. It took 2 weeks for my ear block to clear from that flight.

On another trip, I flew with a pilot who was an extreme "can do" kind of guy. He had a head cold but kept flying anyway, despite many warnings from other pilots. On my flight with him, he experienced severe ear pain on the descent.

We did our best to make the descent extremely gradual, so much so that we had to circle our destination airport several times. When we got on the ground, he had blood down the left side of his shirt. It turns out his left eardrum had ruptured from the pressure change and he was unable to fly for two months until it healed. So if you think you have a head cold, make sure you can effectively clear your ears or do not fly!

Defending Against Diseases

Be sure you stay hydrated, take echinacea or other immune support herbs, get lots of Vitamin C, and use a decongestant. If you have never tried using a warm nasal rinse (such as NeilMed Sinus Rinse or a neti pot), I highly recommend it. It rinses out your sinus cavity with a saline solution, hydrating the tissues as well as removing dust, germs, and exudates. A sinus spray such as Afrin is a good way to temporarily relieve swollen sinus cavities so you can fly. Wear gloves, avoid touching your face, sneeze and cough into tissues or elbow. You should also wash your hands often and possibly wear a mouth and nose mask if you are concerned about airborne contagions.

If you are wary about bacteria or viruses, prepare your body ahead of time with the previously mentioned techniques (hydration, immune support, nutrition). Get plenty of quality sleep, drink lots of water, take 1000mg of vitamin C or more, perhaps make a green smoothie or greens powder mix, take echinacea or zinc, use B vitamins for energy and to reduce stress, and bring lots of disinfectant wipes with you.

Thousands of people transit these airports and airplanes daily, so wash those hands after touching elevators and escalators, ticket counters, and gate waiting area chairs. Typically germs are spread directly from person to person, or from items exposed to an infected individual. Other areas you may want to wipe down are aircraft armrests, tray tables, controller buttons, seat backs, seat pockets, headsets, lavatory faucets, and even the things that the flight attendant hands you.

Remember that flight attendants take credit cards, empty cups, and a variety of items from other passengers. They have already been exposed to many germs, so they have strong immune systems. But if any of the passengers are sick, those germs can be passing around the cabin.

Anti-Clotting Techniques

Blood clots seem to be on the rise and are getting a lot of attention lately. Partly this is due to thick blood. Thinner blood allows the body to better oxygenate the blood, with little detrimental coagulation. The organs function more efficiently allowing for better immunity and energy.

We want to keep circulation and hydration going while we are in flight. Each hour, get up and walk around the jet if you can. Keeping the blood moving through our bodies and having our hearts pumping strongly will help reduce the chances of forming any blood clots. Having a sedentary lifestyle whether at home, hotel, or on the jet is simply not good for any of us, physically or emotionally.

One day I was sitting in the back of a twin aisle 767 as a passenger. I kept seeing the same man walk past me every 5 minutes or so. After the third time, I realized he was using the jet aisles as a circular walking track! He'd walk up one aisle, cross over, down the other aisle. What a great idea! I saw as I watched that he was respectful and courteous to his fellow passengers and to the flight attendants, not interfering with their duties.

If you're not that bold, another technique to keep the blood flowing is by using clenching and stretching techniques. Start with your toes and feet, calf and shins. Tighten them strongly and hold it for a count of 10. Do this five times in a row every hour that you are in flight. Then, progressively move the clenching up your body toward your heart by doing legs, then thighs, then buttocks. Follow this with the tummy and back clenches, then your shoulders, and arms.

Finish with a slow head roll to stretch out the neck. This not only gets the blood flowing, but it releases lactic acid from your muscles and stretches them. Hey, it sure feels good too!

Biorhythms

Jet lag is a real challenge for all of us who travel across the time zones. Sometimes, we can feel like we have been hit by a semi-truck, then dragged along the ground for a few miles. This is because our bodies need to be in the natural flow of our circadian rhythms.

When we start disrupting this cycle, all sorts of things happen to us biologically. Our brain activity, hormone production, cell regeneration, and digestion are all examples of things that are affected. Crossing time zones create confusion to your body, since light and darkness occur when your body is not expecting it.

The same applies for having the lights on inside the jet at times when it should be dark and you are usually sleeping, such as when flying late into the evening or all-nighters. Normally, around 9pm in the time zone where you reside, your body responds to the darkness by creating the hormone melatonin. Melatonin acts as a relaxing agent and a powerful antioxidant, which plays an important role in certain types of our DNA.

When flying during extended daylight hours (summertime) or sitting in a well-lit airplane, our melatonin receptors are not activated and our bodies release less melatonin. With the light present, our bodies cannot fully relax and get into the deep sleep needed for rejuvenation. Nor does it allow the digestive or excretory systems to fully shut down for the night.

This is why you will sometimes experience bloating, constipation, or diarrhea when taking an all-night flight across the time zones. The next morning comes too early for a body set to a different clock. If someone is exposed to this continually, such as in off-shift or rotating shift work, it can create a host of maladies. These include depression, irritability, digestive issues, and even personality disorders.

Jet Lag

There are several things that you can do as a traveler to mitigate the effects of jet lag. If you are on a trip that is of a relatively short duration, maybe a couple of days, try to keep your meal times and sleep schedule the same as at home, if possible. For example, if you live in Colorado but fly to New York for business, your body is two hours off. Your 7am in New York is only 5am back home, and your body knows this, so help it out.

Perhaps you can shower the night before instead of in the morning so you can sleep in a little later on the East Coast clock. Perhaps instead of eating breakfast as soon as you wake up, you wait an hour and then eat. When it is time for bed, perhaps you go to bed a little later. If you are on a longer trip or are crossing multiple time zones, slowly ease your body into the new schedule over a few days. Do a few hour increments each day until your body clock is caught up.

Melatonin supplements are another way to help your body adjust. Take natural melatonin in low dosages for short-term use to help get to sleep. Avoid using heavy sleep aid medications, since most consist of sedatives and can leave you groggy. Also be sure to hydrate yourself and get some nutritious food to help your body make the swing and gain optimum performance.

Travel Medicine and Comforts

When you are planning to take a trip on an aircraft, it may help to put together a travel kit. Bring with you an eye mask to help with the sunlight or cabin lights. This will allow your melatonin receptors to think it is dark and release melatonin to help you sleep. If you struggle with dry or tired eyes, you can bring eye drops or gel. Many people like the soft neck pillows that help prevent the classic neck bobbing as you try to sleep sitting up. Some are even inflatable so you can easily store them when not in use.

Good quality earplugs are a must as well. They can block out jet noise, talkative passengers, crying babies, and snoring seatmates. Some people bring noise cancelling headphones to filter out all noises but still be able to listen to video and audio entertainment. As a pilot, I can tell a big difference in my fatigue level when there is constant, inconsistent background noise, such as flying near large metropolitan areas across the country, and when there is not, such as flying over the Pacific to Hawaii. So cancel out the noise pollution as much as you can.

Always bring lots of healthy water with you. You'll have to purchase it after security or bring an empty container that you fill up before boarding. The little 4oz cup that you get from the flight attendants is not nearly enough. Bring some wholesome snacks to keep your blood sugar regulated. Wanda Collins, my friend and fellow pilot for a major airline says, "It's really important to keep your energy up. You never want to be dehydrated or run down, especially when you travel."

If you ever feel light-headed, woozy, or weak, tell the flight attendants so they can get you juice or a snack, medical oxygen, or medical help depending on the seriousness of your symptoms.

You never know when you'll unexpectedly be staying the night at an airport or hotel. Be sure to have something to read or do to keep your brain comfortably engaged while you travel. Pack a carry-on emergency kit with a change of underwear, toothbrush, toothpaste, soap, deodorant, and brush (don't forget the TSA rules!). Also bring any medications you are taking in that kit. In some cases, your checked luggage will not be unloaded and released to you for a delayed or rescheduled flight.

We Are All In This Together

My final advice on travel health is to be open. Much as we may love the adventure and experience, traveling can also be frustrating and uncomfortable, especially if you are dealing with some serious life circumstances. Instead of closing down and introverting, I am asking you to open yourself up and make eye contact with the people around you. Even giving a small smile can make a huge difference for someone.

It is so much healthier for us to be light in spirit and to laugh than it is to be stressed and stern. Letting your guard down and allowing others in can result in some of the most educational, enlightening, and connecting experiences. Many times in my life, I have ridden in the passenger cabin and I really feel like magic happened. When I consciously chose to be vulnerable, I was amazed. Life struggles were eased, questions were answered, emotions were shared, and deals were made, simply by being available.

One of my favorite sayings is by Josephine Billings - "To the whole world, you may be one person, but to one person, you may be the whole world." Life is made up of a million moments, and we can choose how we want to spend them. Thank you for the shared experiences and lifetime privilege of flying with you!

Come fly with me again at CaptainLaura.com, Facebook, Twitter, Instagram, LinkedIn, Google +, and Youtube!

Editor: Demi Rasmussen

Cover Concept: Laura Einsetler

Photographer: Corinne Alavekios

Website and cover designer: Kevin Mayer, Bear Creek Web LLC